Hall block at Christchurch, Dorset

THE CASTLES
OF WESSEX

Mike Salter

FOLLY PUBLICATIONS

ACKNOWLEDGEMENTS

Most of the photographs in this book were taken by the author. Other views are reproduced from old postcards in the author's collection. The author also drew the map and the plans, which are on scales of 1:400, 1:800, 1:2000, and 1:4000, like those in the other castle books in this series. Thanks are due Marjorie Salter, who checked proofs and Helen Thomas, who did the driving on several field trips during the winter of 2001-2. Kate Miles provided material upon which some of the plans are based, Mr A.J.Cook provided the two pictures of Ludgershall Castle, whilst the two photos of Calshot Castle and the views of Hurst on page 41 and Yarmouth on page 68 are reproduced from a collection of photographs lent by Andrew Tanner.

AUTHOR'S NOTES

This series of books (see full list inside back cover) are intended as portable field guides giving as much information and illustrative material as possible in volumes of modest size, weight and price. As a whole the series aims to make information available about less well known buildings. The aim in the castle books has been to mention, where the information is known to the author, owners or custodians of buildings who erected or altered parts of them, and those who were the first or last of a line to hold an estate, an important office, or a title. Those in occupation at the time of dramatic events such as sieges or royal visits are often also named. Other owners and occupants whose lives had little effect on the condition of the buildings are generally not mentioned, nor are ghost stories, myths and legends.

The books are intended to be used in conjunction with the Ordnance Survey 1:50,000 scale maps. Grid references are given in the gazetteer, together with a coded system indicating which sites can be visited or easily seen by the public from adjacent open spaces which is explained on page 104. Generally speaking, maps will be required to find the lesser known sites and earthworks hidden in woods and fields.

Each level of a building is called a storey in this book, the basement being the first storey with its floor near courtyard level unless specifically mentioned as otherwise.

Measurements given in the text and scales on the plans are in metres, the unit used by the author for all measurements taken on site. Although the buildings were designed using feet the metric scales are much easier to use and are now standard amongst academics working on historic buildings and ancient sites. For those who feet a need to make a conversion 3 metres is almost 10 feet. Unless specifically mentioned as otherwise all dimensions are external at or near ground level, but above the plinth if there is one. On the plans the original work is shown black, post 1800 work is stippled and alterations and additions of intermediate periods are hatched.

ABOUT THE AUTHOR

Mike Salter is 48 and has been a professional writer and publisher since he went on the Government Enterprise Allowance Scheme for unemployed people in 1988. He is particularly interested in the planning and layout of medieval buildings and has a huge collection of plans of castles and churches he has measured during tours (mostly by bicycle and motorcycle) throughout all parts of the British Isles since 1968. Wolverhampton born and bred, Mike now lives in an old cottage beside the Malvern Hills. His other interests include walking, maps, railways, board games, morris dancing, playing percussion instruments and calling dances with a folk group.

Copyright 2002 by Mike Salter. First published March 2002.
Folly Publications, Folly Cottage, 151 West Malvern Rd, Malvern, Worcs, WR14 4AY
Printed by Aspect Design, 89 Newtown Rd, Malvern, Worcs, WR14 2PD

Odiham Castle

CONTENTS

A map of sites described appears inside the front cover.

INTRODUCTION

The name of this book is rather a misnomer. Wessex was a kingdom during the Saxon period and castles were only introduced to England by the Normans. A few castles were built by Normans living in England during the time of the penultimate Saxon king Edward the Confessor, but none of these were in Wessex and to all intents and purposes the story of castle building in this part of England starts with Duke William of Normandy's successful invasion of 1066. Having taken the English crown William granted estates to his followers in return for specified periods of military service. The Norman lords or barons then turn gave units of land called manors to their knights, again in turn for military service, this system being known as feudalism. The thin veneer of land-owning Normans consolidated their fragile hold on the land by constructing castles serving as residences, strongholds and as symbols of lordly rank. The Romans and Saxons built purely military forts and defences around settlements but the Normans introduced the idea of powerful individuals erecting fortresses to serve as their residences and as the administrative centres of groups of manors. The Domesday Book survey commissioned by William I in 1086 to record who was holding what land and what it was considered to be worth records a few castles in the four counties of Dorset, Hampshire, Somerset and Wiltshire and the existence of others is implied. These castles were generally not of mortared stone but of earth and wood, materials which allowed a more rapid construction and some prefabrication.

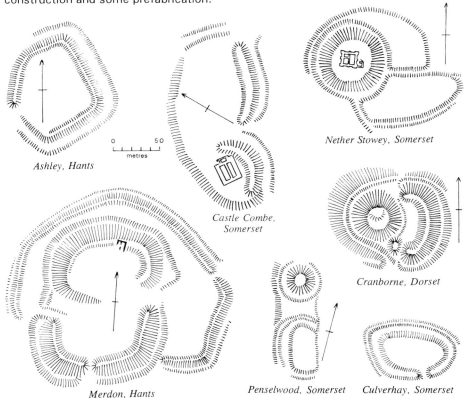

Ashley, Hants

0   50
metres

Castle Combe, Somerset

Nether Stowey, Somerset

Cranborne, Dorset

Merdon, Hants

Penselwood, Somerset   Culverhay, Somerset

Plans of Norman Castle Earthworks

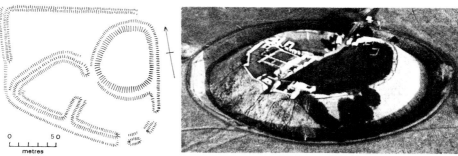

Plan of Barley Pound at Crondall, Hants

Old Sarum, Wiltshire

Late 11th century castles often had a high mound or motte made from material taken out of the surrounding ditch and having on top the lord's residence in the form of a two or three storey wooden tower surrounded by a palisade. The mound summit was reached by a ramp up from a forecourt or bailey in which were sited a range of stores, workshops, a hall and various apartments, plus a chapel, all originally built out of wood with roofs of shingles or thatch. Cranborne in Dorset has a good example of a castle of this type which was never rebuilt in stone. An alternative form to the mound was a ringwork with a high rampart surrounding the lord's house. Castles of these types continued to be built until the late 12th century and can only be precisely dated when there is a record of their foundation or excavation evidence, either of which are lacking for many of the sites described in this book.

The keep at Corfe Castle, Dorset

The basic design of these castles varied according to the terrain and resources available. Natural landscape features were utilised where possible, hillocks and spurs being shaped and heightened into steep-sided and level-topped mottes, as at Dunster, whilst baileys were omitted or duplicated and made whatever size and shape local circumstances dictated. At Old Sarum and Bincknoll Iron Age camps were utilised to form outer enclosures whilst at Merdon older earthworks were ignored and a completely new scheme imposed on the site. At Porchester a former Roman fort still remained defensible and served as the outer bailey of the castle built in one corner. A royal castle was similarly built in a corner of the Roman walled town at Winchester. Royal strongholds and castles a caput or chief seat of great lords tend to have multiple enclosures and outworks whilst the smaller castles built by their knights might only be a single ringwork or a modest motte and bailey. In many cases the earthworks have become worn down over the centuries or deliberately levelled either as a form of demilitarisation or simply to facilitate a different usage of the land.

Plan of tower at Merdon

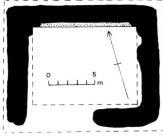

Keep plan, Marshwood, Dorset

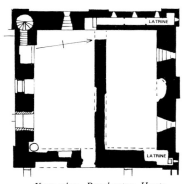

Keep plan, Porchester, Hants

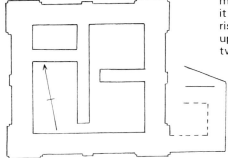

Keep plan, Nether Stowey, Somerset

Wooden buildings are vulnerable to accidental or malicious destruction by fire and eventually rot when in constant contact with damp soil. Although structures of timber remained an important element in the defences of most castles up until the 14th century, the most important parts would gradually be replaced by walls and towers of mortared stone. Only Corfe, a natural hill which hardly required earthworks, seems to have been fortified in stone in the first two or three decades after the Norman Conquest of 1066, the inner bailey having fragments of a massive wall, and the west bailey containing parts of an early hall, whilst an outer bailey was walled in stone by the 1130s.

There are quite a number of structures thought to date from Henry I's reign (1100-1135), although few can be accurately dated. The king himself is thought to have built the square tower keeps at Corfe, Porchester, Old Sarum, Wareham, and perhaps that at Winchester, and his nephew the bishop of Winchester built a keep at Taunton. Nothing remains visible of the keep at Wareham, and only the lowest parts revealed by excavation remain of those at Bristol, Nether Stowey, Taunton, and Winchester, and of two others, Castle Cary (now covered up again) and Nether Stowey, which also probably existed by 1140, so we can only guess at their original internal arrangements. The keeps at Corfe and Porchester are lofty structures with evidence of four storeys, although that at Porchester was heightened later and originally only had two levels, with a hall and chamber side-by-side over two dark basement rooms. The fourth storey at Corfe was only created much later within the former roof-space, for it was normal in these keeps for the walls to rise above, and thus protect, the roofs. The upper rooms had round headed windows of two lights. At each keep a stair led up in a forebuilding to an entrance at second storey level. Forebuildings often contained chapels, and traces of one remain at Porchester, where there was also a rectangular court with a square corner bastion and a gatehouse. Corfe and Old Sarum each had a forebuilding and latrine block added later, whilst that at Porchester was rebuilt several times.

Apart from Taunton, Bishop Henry of Winchester had several other seats, including Bishop's Waltham, Merdon, where substantial earthworks and one tower remain, and Wolvesey at Winchester, where he fortified his palace with a gatehouse, curtain wall and moat and built a second hall block, a predecessor having already built another block back in c1110. Bishop Roger of Sarum (Salisbury) was also a great builder, responsible for the vanished mighty fortress at Devizes which had an aisled hall and great keep, and the castle at Sherborne with an outer wall with several flanking towers set around a palace with ranges around a central court and the bishop's own chamber within a massive keep. Three of the towers on the outer wall at Sherborne served as gatehouses. One of the gateways at Wolvesey was of a more advanced form with two square towers flanking a central passageway, although this structure may not have been built until the 1160s. Bishop Roger provided himself with a palace beside his cathedral at Old Sarum and supervised the addition of a palace within the adjacent royal castle, of which he eventually became custodian. The palace in the castle was similar to that at Sherborne, with four ranges including a hall, upper and lower chapels and private rooms set around a central court. The Earl of Devon's castle at Carisbrooke on the Isle of Wight had a large stone-walled bailey by 1136, and a keep of a different type, a shell wall around a small court perched on top of the motte. Nothing now remains standing of later keeps of this type at Marlborough and Southampton, and the latter has even lost its great motte.

Christchurch and Bishop's Waltham both have hall blocks of the 1160s. The latter was at ground level until remodelled in the 14th century. The former, which is comparatively complete, has an upper floor hall and chamber with several round-headed windows of two lights. Christchurch also has a tower keep of uncertain date with the rare feature of the corners chamfered off. Porchester also had several stone domestic buildings of the late 12th century. The lower parts of the block containing constable's hall remain but the main hall and chamber were swept away by successive rebuildings during the 14th century. Taunton too has remains of an early hall and chamber, possibly even older than the keep. Carisbrooke also has some remains of a late 12th century hall block.

The keep at Sherborne, Dorset

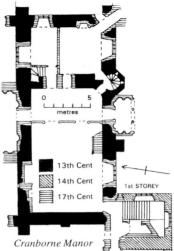

■	13th Cent
▨	14th Cent
▤	17th Cent

1st STOREY

The SW side of Corfe Castle   *Cranborne Manor*

The castles of Dorset, Hampshire, Somerset and Wiltshire saw much action during the civil wars of King Stephen's reign (1135-54). Several instances are known of siege works being erected by one side or the other to blockade a hostile garrison. A good example survives just west of the main castle at Corfe. A number of other fresh castles were also erected during the conflict. After Henry II came to the throne in 1154 the king tightened up on the control of castles. Those held by barons or bishops of doubtful loyalty were seized and either retained as royal castles or demolished. Bishop Henry of Winchester's many seats certainly suffered from some dismantling. Records of royal expenditure are more complete from this reign onwards and Henry is known to have spent small sums on many of the castles, although the main ones seem to have been regarded as adequately fortified and Henry II's main military works all lie in other parts of England. King John (1199-1216) refortified the two outer baileys at Corfe in stone and built a palace called the Gloriette in the inner bailey. The walls were flanked by a series of D-shaped towers and there was an octagonal tower at the acute angle at the end of the west bailey. The keep of the king's new castle at Odiham was also octagonal. Only earthworks remain of John's hunting seat at Powerstock, but the much altered shell remains of his hall and chamber block at Cranborne, and a very defaced tower at Ludgershall which is though to have acted as a solar tower, or mini-keep containing his private apartments. Hardly anything now remains of a once important baronial castle of this period at Bridgwater. From this period onwards the construction of embattled secular buildings required a royal licence, and the records of such licences help to date many later buildings.

Henry III was a prolific builder and also liked his comforts. We have quite detailed information about the halls, chambers, chapels, and other buildings that he erected at Ludgershall and Marlborough, although the only remains of all this are footings at Ludgershall. Of his work on the defences at Winchester there remains just the base of one tower, but his splendid aisled hall of the 1220s has survived almost intact with just minor alterations. Parts of the outer defences at Corfe were also built by Henry III, although the work continued under his son Edward I (1272-1307). There are no standing remains of the important castles built during his reign at Trowbridge and Mere, the latter built by the king's brother Richard, but low lengths of walling with D-shaped towers and the lower parts of gateways flanked by such towers remain in the Somerset castles of Dunster and Stogursey.

By the early 14th century many of the older castles were in a decayed state and the minor earthwork sites had mostly been abandoned. Porchester got a new lease of life since it was used as a royal port. Edward II and Edward III did much work on the apartments, only for Richard II to almost completely rebuild them in the 1390s. They remain much as he left them, just lacking their roofs and floors. Firearms gradually came into use during the late 14th century. The town defences of Southampton contain gunports possibly as early as the 1360s, and others of c1380 appear in a tower at Porchester and in the circular turrets of the barbican gatehouse at Carisbrooke. Edward III also carried out much work on the castle at Southampton, a new keep being built on the motte. At Wells the bishop's palace, with remains of two 13th century hall blocks, was unfortified until provided in the 1340s with a curtain wall with corner towers, a gatehouse and a wet moat which are still almost intact. Farleigh Hungerford was likewise an unfortified house until a rectangular court with round corner towers and a twin-towered gatehouse was added in the 1370s. There only fragments of two towers now stand above the foundations. Nothing now remains standing of a fortified manor house at Chideock, but a fine block of still-roofed apartments remains at Woodsford. This structure once had five towers, although only one remains. Wardour is a very remarkable building of the 1390s with apartments set in ranges around a small hexagonal court. One range is built wider to accommodate the hall and here appear the only flanking projections, two rectangular wings. The other corners had only bartizans at the top. Nunney is a more modest but still impressive structure of the 1370s, with just a single rectangular block with private rooms within circular towers at the corners set within a wet moat. The towers had an additional storey within a machicolated parapet. As at Wardour there was an outer court on minimal defensive strength to enclose all the outbuildings.

At Bishop's Waltham the apartments were dramatically remodelled in the late 14th century with tall new windows with transoms, and in the early 15th century the tower containing the bishop's bedroonm was heightened by one storey. Other 15th century work includes the impressive outer gatehouse at Dunster and an outer court with round towers and a square gatehouse at Farleigh Hungerford, both of the 1420s, plus the inner gatehouse and an adjacent range at Taunton, and the small pentagonal court at Rufus on the Isle of Portland which contains circular gunports.

Yarmouth Castle

Chapel and SE Tower at Farleigh Hungerford, Somerset

Bailey wall at Southampton

Nunney Castle

Hampshire contains two houses for which licences to crenellate were issued as late as Henry VIII's reign. At Titchfield the former abbey was converted into a mansion with an impressive gatehouse with cross-loops in the corner turrets. Basing House had several gatehouses of this type and was an enormous mansion quite strongly protected by the older earthworks surrounding it. However, these are exceptions, and in the south of England by Henry VIII's reign the domestic and military elements combined in medieval castles had gone their separate ways in the form of unfortified Tudor houses on the one hand and the purely military forts built by the state to defend the south coast against invasion. Hampshire contains a high concentration of such forts, built in the period 1537 to 1547 to protect the approaches to Henry VIII's naval base at Portsmouth and the important trading port of Southampton. These forts are generally set round down at sea level and consisted of a central tower or keep containing accommodation for soldiers and gunners, surrounded by open platforms for mounting cannon. At Southsea the central keep is square, at Netley it is rectangular, and there the platforms also had rectangular or triangular forms, whilst at Calshot and Hurst the keeps are circular, Calshot having a circular surrounding chemise, whilst at Hurst the outer platforms are built on a tri-lobed plan. Three forts in Dorset all have a gun-platform on the seaward side only of the keep. At Portland the keep is circular and the platform is fan shaped, whilst Sandsfoot had a polygonal gun platform and a rectangular main body, and the blockhouse on Brownsea Island had a square main building. On the Isle of Wight the forts at Sandown and Yarmouth had square enclosures with a range of buildings on one side, an open platform on the other side, beyond an open court, whilst the landward sides were flanked in each case by a single arrowhead shaped bastion of the most up-to-date type. Several much larger bastions of this type were built by Elizabeth I around the castle of Carisbrooke and the town of Portsmouth.

Southsea Castle

Bishop's Waltham Palace, Hampshire

In the medieval period castle walls of rubble were often limewashed both inside and out, making them look very different to the way they appear today. Dressed stones around windows and doorways would be left uncovered. Domestic rooms would have had murals of biblical, historical or heroic scenes mostly painted in red, yellow and black. Wall hangings decorated with the same themes or heraldry gradually became more common from the 14th century onwards. Although used in churches and chapels, glass was expensive and uncommon in secular buildings before the 15th century, so windows were originally closed with wooden shutters. As a result rooms were dark when the weather was too cold or wet for them to be opened for light and ventilation. Large openings in the outer walls sometimes had iron bars or projecting grilles even if high above ground level. Living rooms usually had fireplaces although some halls had central hearths with the smoke escaping through louvres in the roof. Latrines were provided within the thickness of the outer walls. .

Old Sarum Castle from the cathedral site

Sherborne Castle

Furnishings in castles were sparse up until the 15th century although the embrasures of upper storey windows sometimes have built-in stone seats. Lords with several castles tended to circulate around them administering their manorial courts and consuming agricultural produce on the spot. Seats belonging to great lords could be left almost empty when they and their families were not in residence. For much of their lives castles gradually crumbled away with only a skeleton staff to administer the estates. Servants travelled with their lords and sometimes also portable furnishings such as rugs, wall hangings, cooking vessels and bedding, all kept in wooden chests. The lord and his immediate family plus honoured guests and senior household officials would enjoy a fair degree of privacy by the late 13th century, having their own rooms. Servants and retainers enjoyed less comfort and privacy, sharing of beds and communal sleeping in and places that were warm being common.

Scattered across the four counties, but most numerous on low lying sites, are moated platforms marking the sites of former manor houses, most of which were built of perishable materials and were not otherwise fortified. The majority of the moats date from the 13th and 14th centuries and commonly have a ditch about 10m wide and up to 3m deep surrounding a quadrangular platform up to 60m long. The few moats with round platforms may be a transitional type related to mottes. Few moats in SW England have been excavated or properly surveyed so their history and purpose can ofton only be surmised. The digging of ditches was not regulated like the construction of embattled walls since moated houses were status symbols of the landed classes and not really military sites, although some were garrisoned during the Civil War. Moats were valued as scenic features and served to keep out vagrants and wild animals and keep in the children, servants and domestic animals of a household.

Bishop's Palace at Wells

Corfe Castle, showing the dramatic effects of slighting.

Many of the castles in Hampshire, Dorset, Somerset and Wiltshire played a part in the Civil War of the 1640s. Improved cannon had made lofty stone walls and towers redundant militarily, and some castles like Nunney only withstood bombardment for a day or two, yet others withstood lengthy sieges before they were captured. Basing and Corfe in particular were closely besieged for many months and Corfe proved a very tough nut to crack. After Parliament was finally victorious in 1646 many castles were destroyed to prevent them being used again as fortresses. Destruction at Basing and Devizes was particularly thorough, but quite a lot of walling still remains a Corfe, even if thrown at all angles by gunpowder and undermining.

The 16th century artillery forts at Calshot, Hurst, Portland, Southsea, and Yarmouth remained in military use until they were handed over for preservation as ancient monuments in recent times, Southsea being a museum run by Portsmouth Council and the others in the care of English Heritage. Two others, Brownsea and Netley, had become private dwellings by the late 18th century. All of these seven forts have been adapted and extended over the years. At Dunster only the defences seem to have been slighted and the domestic buildings have remained in use, and at Taunton and Winchester the great halls managed to survive in use as a court rooms. At Wells part of the accommodation is in use and part is ruined, but the defensive enceinte remains remarkably intact. The hunting lodge at Cranborne was made into a new mansion as early as the beginning of the 17th century, and the principal range at Woodsford also remains in use, although its original roof and battlements have long gone. Porchester remained in use until the 19th century and the keep is still roofed, although the other buildings are ruined. Carisbrooke also long remained in use as the residence of the governor of the Isle of Wight and has a mixture of roofed and ruined buildings. Carisbrooke and Portchester are in the care of English Heritage, as are other preserved ruins at Bishop's Waltham, Farleigh Hungerford, Ludgershall, Nunney, Old Sarum, Sherborne, Titchfield, Wardour, and Wolvesey. Dunster is maintained by the National Trust, as are the ruins at Corfe, whilst parts of Stogursey and Woodsford are holiday homes in the care of the Landmark Trust, and Taunton is the museum of the Somerset Archaeological Society. Little remains to be seen of the other castles apart from minor ruins and earthworks which in some places are quite substantial.

GAZETTEER OF CASTLES IN DORSET

BRIDPORT CASTLE

There are no remains of the castle surrendered in 1149 to Henry, Duke of Normandy. The town was protected by a ditch on the one side not enclosed by rivers.

BROWNSEA CASTLE   SZ 029876

This building, also once known as Branksea Castle, lies by the quay on the east side of Brownsea Island. As built c1545 by Henry VIII it comprised a blockhouse 13m square over walls almost 3m thick with a battered plinth towards the ditch on the landward sides, whilst the east side was covered by a polygonal gun platform (now a garden terrace). The main building was entered by a doorway on the south, where the main room lay. Two smaller rooms lay in the northern part and there was a gun platform on top. The cost of building and manning the blockhouse was borne by the town of Poole but Queen Elizabeth later agreed to provide new guns, one inventory of this period mentioning eight of them, with 12 hundredweight of powder. The fort held a Parliamentary garrison during the 1640s but saw no action. It was subsequently occupied by William Benson, and then in 1786 passed to Charles Sturt. By 1774 the original building, much of which survives in the basement, had been remodelled into a four storey castellated structure with Venetian windows. The NW front dates from shortly after the island was sold to Sir Charles Chad in 1817. The other sides were rebuilt after Colonel William Petrie Waugh purchased the island in 1852, but were partly refaced in red brick after a fire in 1896, when the owner was Kenneth Balfour. Although most of the island is in National Trust ownership the castle is used as a recreation and conference centre for the staff of John Lewis stores.

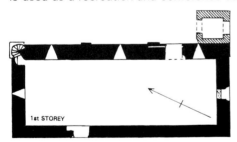
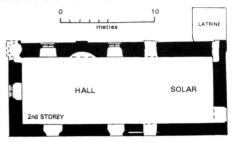

Plans of the hall block at Christchurch

The keep at Christchurch

Hall window at Christchurch

CHIDEOCK CASTLE   SY 424931   F

Only a moated platform now remains of a castle which Sir John Cradock was licensed by Richard II to fortify after a French raid on Weymouth in 1377. The castle was captured by a Parliamentary force in March 1643, but was recovered by the Royalists in December 1644. A hundred prisoners and munitions including three barrels of powder were taken when the castle was surrendered to Parliament in July 1645. Colonel Ceely, Governor of Lyme Regis, was then ordered to destroy it. The last remaining building, a ruined gatehouse depicted by the Buck brothers on an engraving of 1733, was destroyed in 1741. The building was of three storeys with large upper windows of two lights with transoms. The engraving shows two walls still standing, with three of the octagonal corner turrets, which rose one stage higher. No details are known of the design of the rest of the building.

CHRISTCHURCH CASTLE   SZ 163926   F

Nothing remains of the ramparts of the burh or fortified town built in the ninth century by King Alfred. The castle existed by 1147-8, when it was captured by Walter de Pikney. It was probably founded by Richard de Redvers early in Henry I's reign and remained with the Redvers family until 1293, when their heiress Isabel de Fortibus, handed it over to Edward I. The ruined hall block beside the River Avon was probably built in the 1160s, whilst the keep lying 65m to the west is of uncertain date. The mound is no more than earth piles against the lower part of the keep, which is built on virgin soil, so it is not a true Norman motte and may be as late as the 13th century. The nature of the bailey defences and its other buildings are unknown. It now contains a bowling green. Christchurch was given in 1330 by Edward III to William Montagu, created Earl of Salisbury in 1337. It passed to Isabel, wife of George Duke of Clarence. Their son Edward, Earl of Lincoln was executed by Henry VII in 1499 and their daughter Lady Margaret Pole was executed by Henry VIII in 1541. The castle was sold to the Arundell family in 1601 and was surrendered to Parliament without a siege in 1644, 400 prisoners being taken. Two attempts by the Royalists to recapture it failed. In 1650 the Governor of Southampton was ordered to demolish the castle, although the job was only finished in the summer of 1651, following complaints that cannon were lying there unguarded.

The keep measures 12m by 14m over walls 3m thick and shows evidence of two storeys above mound summit level. Very unusually, the corners of the building were chamfered off. The hall block is better preserved and measures 22m by 10.7m, the east wall facing the river being 1.8m thick and the other walls 1.4m thick. It contained a hall and solar set either side of a passage onto which opened an upper doorway with a drawbar slot. The hall has a fireplace with a circular stack in the east wall, and five good windows of two rounded-headed lights, one facing north and two each to the east and west. The solar has no fireplace and had only a single-light east window, but is provided with a passage to a latrine in the upper part of a 13th century turret at the SE corner. This room also has another doorway at the SW corner. The broken down NE corner contained a spiral staircase down to a basement room with two narrow loops facing the river, one more facing north, and a doorway with a drawbar slot facing west. The room under the solar has one loop and a remodelled doorway with a drawbar slot facing towards the river. Above was a another roof in the roof. See page 1.

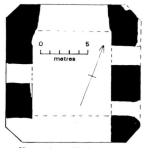

Keep plan, Christchurch

The Gloriette at Corfe

CORFE CASTLE   SY 957823   O

It is generally accepted that the entry in Domesday Book recording the building of the castle of Wareham on land in the manor of Kingston which the king (William I) had obtained by an exchange with Shaftsbury Abbey actually refers to Corfe. The wall of the inner bailey and the hall in the west bailey are assumed to have been built by this time. The hall seems to have replaced a Saxon timber building and King Edward is thought to have been murdered in this vicinity in 978. Henry I is thought to have built the keep and an outer bailey. His brother Robert, Duke of Normandy, who was captured in 1106 and then spent the rest of his life in confinement, is assumed to have been kept within the keep. In 1139 Baldwin de Redvers took possession of Corfe after landing at Wareham. King Stephen besieged the castle but withdrew on hearing of the imminent landing of the Empress Matilda and Robert of Gloucester, his main adversaries. On the West Hill 0.3km west of the castle is an earthwork called The Rings which is thought to have been built as a siegework during this campaign, although since an old tithe map refers to it as Cromwell's Battery, it may have also been used by besiegers during the Civil War. It comprises a ringwork 50m across and up to 4m high with a bailey 60m wide extending 50m down the slope to the SSE.

There is not much evidence that Henry II took much interest in Corfe, but King John was a frequent visitor and is known to have spent over £1400 on improving both the accommodation and the defences. The palace known as the Gloriette in the inner ward and the walls and towers of the west bailey are thought to be of the first half of John's reign, whilst the great ditch below the keep and the ditch isolating the south end of the outer bailey are of 1207-14. In 1214 there is a record of the sheriff of Gloucester being ordered to send down to Corfe two stone-throwing siege-engines. At the time of John's death in 1216 his young daughter Eleanor was living at Corfe under the custody of Peter de Mauley, Sheriff of Dorset. Eleanor later married Simon de Montfort and their younger son Amauri was imprisoned at the castle by Edward after being captured in 1275 whilst escorting his sister Eleanor, who was destined to be the bride of the Welsh prince Llewelyn ap Gryffudd.

Corfe Castle from the south

During Henry III's long reign over £1000 was spent on works at Corfe. The keep was repaired in 1235, when two walls were also built to replace sections of palisading in the outer defences. In 1244 the keep was whitewashed externally and timber supplied for the king's chapel. The middle gatehouse between the outer bailey and the west bailey is also of that period. Edward I was also responsible for much work on the castle. The outer gatehouse was built in the 1280s, and work was done to the Butavant tower at the western corner of the west bailey and to another tower which probably stood in the inner ward SE corner, whilst in the early 1290s the Gloriette was repaired and the keep heightened. Edward II was briefly held at Corfe in the custody of Sir John Maltravers after his deposition in 1326. The castle was said to lack arms and provisions in 1327 and remained neglected until repairs were undertaken prior to a visit by Edward III. A new tower was built in the SE corner of the inner ward by Richard II in 1377-8. John Beaufort, Earl of Somerset was made constable of the castle in 1397, and this office remained with his heirs until Henry Beaufort, Duke of Somerset was attainted by the newly crowned Edward IV in 1461. His brother Richard was made constable, although then only a boy of ten.

In 1496 Henry VII visited the castle and obtained a grant of £2000 from Parliament for repairs to make the place a suitable residence for the king's mother, Margaret, Countess of Richmond, although there is no certain evidence she ever lived in the castle. Queen Elizabeth I sold the castle in 1572 to Sir Christopher Hatton. There still survives a very informative survey and plan made by Hatton's steward Ralph Treswell in 1586. The plan shows cannon in the outer bailey just south of the great ditch, a Spanish invasion then being anticipated. Sir Christopher's nephew and heir Sir William Hatton gave the castle to his wife Lady Elizabeth Cecil. She later married Lord Chief Justice Coke and in 1635 they sold the castle to Sir John Bankes.

South end of Corfe Castle

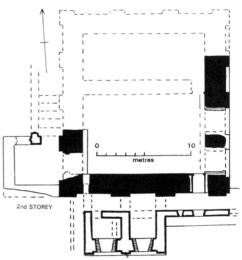

The keep at Corfe   *Corfe: plan of keep*

Sir John Bankes was Chief Justice of the Common Pleas and was in attendance on Charles I when the Civil War began in 1642. By May 1643 Parliamentary forces had taken possession of most of Dorset and Corfe was being blockaded. A truce was made under which Lady Bankes agreed to hand over four small cannon within the castle, after which the blockade was not maintained as tightly as before and she was able to provision the place and thus held out during a six week siege during the summer. Sir John died at Oxford in December 1644 and by the autumn of 1645 the castle was being besieged again by Colonel Bingham and Colonel Pickering. In February 1646 a Royalist Colonel managed to capture the Governor of Wareham and to get through the besiegers lines and into the castle. They offer Lady Bankes a chance to escape with them but she turned it down. Later that month a Parliamentary force managed to enter the outer bailey at night disguised as Royalist reinforcements and with the aid of treachery from an officer of the garrison. The governor was then forced to surrender the castle the next day and thirty Parliamentary prisoners within it were freed. The castle was then thoroughly slighted under the supervision of Captain Hughes of Lulworth. Lady Bankes eventually got the family estates restored to her upon payment of a very heavy fine. His son Sir Ralph Bankes built a new mansion at Kingston Lacy. The Bankes family handed over both the Kingston Lacy estate and the ruins at Corfe to the National Trust in 1981.

A line of hills across the Isle of Purbeck is broken by two valleys creating an isolated hill with steep slopes all around except at the SE end. A stream runs in the western valley and the main road and railway from Swanage in the more steeply sided eastern valley. The inner ward on the highest part of the hill measures about 40m wide by 80m long and is pear-shaped with the pointed end facing west. It ended at that end in a bastion which in the 16th century was filled up with earth to make an artillery platform. This has now gone since the section of the 3m thick 11th century curtain wall which enclosed it on the south has been destroyed. The bastion flanked the gateway in the now mostly destroyed NW section of the curtain wall.

Filling much of the western part of the inner ward, and adjoining the south wall is the keep of c1100-10. It measured 19.6m by 17.4m over walls 2.2m thick above the plinth and had pilaster buttresses at the corners and set along the sides so as to divide the east and west walls into four bays and north and south walls into three bays. The north wall lies in pieces on the ground and other parts are reduced to their leaning lower parts, but most of the south wall with the SW corner and the third bay from the south of the eastern wall still stand four storeys high, the stages being marked externally by chamfered offsets. The keep was divided by a crosswall and originally contained two dark basement rooms and two storeys above consisting of hall on the south and a chamber on the north, but the southern basement chamber was subdivided at some time, and in the 13th century a fourth storey was created within the former roof space. At that level the building had a blind arcade externally and the marks of the original double pitched roof with a central north-south gully can be clearly seen. The keep was entered from a set of steps on the west side up to a porch contained within a slightly later forebuilding. At about the same time a block was added on the south side in such a way as to straddle the curtain wall, the wall-walk of which was carried through it in the form of a lofty vaulted passage. At that level there was a narrow doorway into keep (another was inserted later) and the south extension contain two rooms, one a latrine and the other probably a guard room. The second storey containing the king's private hall and chamber was reached by a stair in the forebuilding up to a round headed doorway into which a smaller Tudor doorway has been inserted. Consequently the chapel, often placed on an upper level in keep forebuildings, was here placed in the southern extension, where a fine doorway to it survives. The chapel has two late 16th century windows facing south and the other windows of the keep were likewise replaced with mullion and transom windows then. A spiral stair in the SE corner led to the later fourth storey and the roof but it does not appear that there were any spiral stairs lower down in the keep.

Fragments of King John's ashlar-faced palace or "Gloriette" fill the SE part of the inner ward, although the actual corner was occupied by a tower built in the 1370s, whilst to the north was a garden. The palace rooms were arranged around a court and included a kitchen in the destroyed west range. The south range contained a room known as the Long Chamber over a barrel-vaulted undercroft. The east range contained a hall 13.5m long by 6m wide set over a vaulted undercroft so that its five bays of twinned lancet windows could look out over the level of the curtain wall-walk. Externally the bays were divided by pilaster buttresses and there was a chamfered string course at hall floor level and a roll-moulded string course just below the upper windows. The hall was reached by steps contained in a porch up to a doorway at the NW corner. The vaulted room north of it was probably the king's presence chamber and it appears there was another room above. A well lay between here and where a turret was later added to the curtain wall. There are remains of a passage leading NW from the Gloriette towards another building of three storeys with traces of 16th century windows. Projecting from the curtain wall between the keep and the Gloriette is a bastion upon which cannon were mounted. It is not shown on the plan of 1586 and must date from between then and the 1640s.

Corfe Castle from the west

The outer bailey and the west bailey together form a crescent shape 220m long and up to 60m wide. From the outer gatehouse at the SE end the ground slopes steadily uphill so that the west bailey is at a higher level and it was possible for cannon mounted behind a now-destroyed crosswall in the outer bailey to fire out over the defences at the SE end. The D-shaped towers of these two baileys either had backs that were open or were closed with timber, although, except for the northernmost tower of the outer bailey west wall they are shown on the plan of 1586 as though they were roofed buildings. The early 13th century west bailey has a north tower 8m in diameter with the remains of four embrasures for arrow loops at courtyard level. This tower remained occupied for a century after the slighting of 1646 and the west half of this bailey was then adapted as a garden with a new wall closing it off to the east. The acute western corner of the west bailey is filled with a tower which was different from all the others, being an octagon about 11.5m across and of three fully enclosed storeys with stairs on the SE side. It is known as the Butavant Tower, although the 1586 plan labels it as the Dungeon Tower. It had a latrine where the curtain adjoined on the NE side. A postern between here and the north tower was blocked up in the 1640s. A length of the south curtain wall of this bailey (which retains its parapet), together with a very ruined south tower (similar in size and layout to the north tower) was built against the south wall of a late 11th century hall block 7.5m wide and 25m long, in which herringbone masonry and three small windows are visible. Nothing remains of the other original walls, nor anything of the 13th century rebuilding of the block on a larger scale except for part of a crosswall dividing it into a hall with a chamber to the west. The west wall is known to have had three pilaster buttresses. This hall was probably used by the castle constables and appears to have been abandoned before the 1586 map was made.

At the SE end of the west bailey a wall of the 1230s, upon which was a steeply stepped wall-walk communicating with that on the inner ward, runs down the steep slope to a gatehouse of c1250. This building had a U-shaped tower on the NE side and a three-quarter round tower on the other side. The latter has dropped nearly 3m down the hillside as a result of the 1646 slighting. The passageway was closed by a two-leaved door and two portcullises operated from the third storey, from which opened also machicolation slots between the door and outer portcullis. In the SW tower the room at this upper level had a latrine corbelled out over the west side and access by a trap-door in the floor to an unlit chamber, perhaps a prison, between it and the guard room with three arrow loops reached from the entrance passage. Both towers have corbels for a wooden hourding at the top.

The 3m thick SW wall of the outer bailey and three of its flanking towers are thought to belong to c1212-15. The towers are 9m in diameter and each have three arrow loops, two of which flank the walls on each side. In one tower these loops have proved a weak point at which the tower has cracked and slid down the hillside, and the adjacent lengths of wall are also slightly below their original position as a result of being undermined and blown up in 1646. Between the last tower and the middle gatehouse is a thin length of rubble walling of uncertain date. It contains three crossloops and closed off the SW end of the great ditch of 1207. At the south end there is a gap and then a dramatically leaning tower. This tower has a cross-slit to its one remaining arrow loop and is thought to have been built much later in the 13th century along with the outer gatehouse, although it seems strange that this most vulnerable end of the castle appears to have been the last part to be walled in stone, unless there were once older stone-built structures at that end. The gatehouse also leans towards the ditch in front of it, which is crossed by a bridge with four 16th century arches set upon piers of the 1280s. Towards the field the gatehouse has two towers 6m in diameter which are solid at the level of the entrance passage, but which contained rooms each with three loops above, although these are now mostly destroyed. The passage was approached over some sort of drawbridge and was closed by a portcullis and two-leaved door secured with a draw-bar. Against the inner part are slight remains of thinly walled guard rooms with fireplaces.

The east wall of the inner bailey was well defended by natural slopes and was consequently thinner. Part of the wall retains the base of the parapet, with three loops. The 1586 plan shows a narrow stable block projecting from the middle of this side, but this has now been destroyed. The wall was originally probably unflanked but in the late 13th century a 6m diameter tower named after Adam de Plukenet, constable of the castle in 1265-70 (his arms appear on the outer face) was added near the north end, and the open-backed 9m diameter Horseshoe Tower was provided at the SE corner of the bailey. Both towers are of two storeys and better preserved than their western counterparts. North of the Plukenet Tower is a length of 12th century curtain which is all that remains of a stone-walled outer bailey which was mostly destroyed in 1207 when the great ditch was dug out.

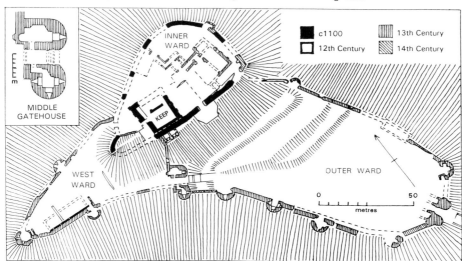

Plans of Corfe Castle

CRANBORNE CASTLE   SU 059127 & 053132

On a ridge above the River Crane SE of the village is a motte rising 8m to a summit
15m across and a crescent-shaped bailey to the east. The bailey entrance lies on the
south side and on the east is a rampart rising 7m above the interior and 15m above
the ditch beyond. The castle probably served as a royal hunting lodge. See page 4.

In 1207 King John built a new lodge west of the church. A buttressed and
embattled building 23.3m by 10.5m over walls 1.5m thick with arrow-loops in the
merlons, it now forms the core of the mansion created from 1608 by Robert Cecil,
1st Earl of Salisbury. The west part contained a hall over a basement, whilst the east
part had an additional third storey upper chamber, providing two private rooms. They
were served by latrines in a SE corner turret which has been obliterated by a SE wing
added by Cecil to match a SW corner tower, probably a 14th century addition, which
he heightened. Part of a lancet remains on the east side and there was a chapel in the
NE corner with an east lancet and a piscina. Where the crosswall meets the south
wall there is a spiral stair in a polygonal turret. The hall is shown roofless in a survey
of 1605 and was later divided into two storeys with mullion-and-transom windows.
A new entrance was made on the south side, the original approach having been from
the north. Cecil added two storey wings at either end but that on the west was
rebuilt by the Fort family in 1647, and the east wing was rebuilt in modern times.

DORCHESTER CASTLE   SY 693909

The prison stands on the site of a castle thought to have been begun by William I in
1070 just outside the Roman town defences. A reference to destroyed houses in
Domesday Book in 1086 implies a newly-built castle, although it is not mentioned
until 1138. Henry II spent £40 on the domestic buildings of the castle in 1185-7.
Until he built a new castle at Powerstock, King John was a frequent visitor to
Dorchester, and spent small sums on the buildings. Edward I sold the castle in 1290
to John Gervase of Bridport, and it later passed to the Franciscan Friars. The castle
had a fine aisled hall with piers of Portesham stone, traces of which survived until the
1790s. Glyde Path Road and Collinton Street lie where its outer ditch once was.
Traces of a medieval ditch and a later ditch (perhaps of the Civil War period) were
found by excavation in 1975. The motte lay in the NW corner of the bailey.

EAST CHELBOROUGH: CASTLE HILL   ST 552054

On the summit of a 180m high hill is an oval motte 9m high lying at the SW corner
of a bailey. A triangulation point lies on the motte. Down by Stake Farm 140m to the
NE at ST 554055 is what appears to be a second worn-down motte.

HOLDITCH COURT   ST 345022

The circular SW corner stair turret stands high of a small square tower of an
embattled house of the Brook family. A section of rampart lies to the south. A 16th
century gatehouse nearby was later extended and made into a house.

LULWORTH CASTLE   SY 855821   O

The castle captured by Robert, Earl of Gloucester in 1142 is thought to have been at
West Lulworth. The rectangular lodge with circular corner towers at East Lulworth
begun in 1608 by Thomas, 3rd Lord Howard of Bindon, was unfortified, although it
held a Royalist garrison in the 1640s. It was inhabited until gutted by fire in 1929.

The keep at Marshwood

MARSHWOOD CASTLE   SY 405977   V

This castle is said to have been built during King John's reign by William de Mandeville. Robert de Mandeville lost most of his lands because of his support for Simon de Montfort in the conflicts of the 1260s and the castle probably soon fell into ruin. A farm lies on the east side of a platform 85m square, the moat of which is now dry except for a pool on the south side. In the SW corner are defaced walls originally about 3m thick of the basement of a keep 17m long by 14.5m wide.

MOHUN CASTLE   ST 472067   V

The churchyard at South Perrot intrudes into a large moated platform.

POOLE TOWN DEFENCES   SZ 010903

Work began on providing the port with defences in 1433, there having been a raid upon it by a combined French and Spanish force in 1405. Further work was done in 1545. A fragment of walling with a corbelled parapet remains in St Clement's Alley.

Portland Castle

PORTLAND CASTLE   SY 685744   E

This fort on the north side of the Isle of Portland was begun by Henry VIII in 1539 and was completed at the end of the following year, having cost almost £5000. The original garrison comprised only a captain, four gunners and two other men, but this could be supplemented by local militia men in times of emergency. Elizabeth I spent over £200 on repairs to the fort in the crisis period leading up to the Armada of 1588. Shortly afterwards Sir Walter Raleigh was made captain of the castle, although he never lived in it. A survey in 1623 recorded the fort as being armed with three culverins, nine demi-culverins, and a saker. It then had a captain, a lieutenant, one porter for each of the inner and outer gateways, a master gunner and several other gunners, although ten men were noted as missing. The moat on the landward side had to be then cleared of undergrowth and protected from the sea by a bank.

During the Civil War the castle quickly came under Parliamentary control, along with the rest of the Isle of Portland. In 1643 a party of Royalists disguised as Parliamentary troops captured the castle in a surprise attack. The castle was attacked by a Parliamentary force in 1644 but a Royalist force managed to relieve the castle. Another attack in 1645 failed and Colonel Thomas Gollop only surrendered on honourable terms in April 1646 to Vice-Admiral William Batten. In 1653 the castle helped protect the anchorage from attack by the Dutch, with whom there was a three day naval battle closeby. In 1681 one of the garrison who acted as the island customs officer was found to be in league with local smugglers. In 1679 there were 16 guns in the castle, all needing new carriages and platforms, but in 1717 this number was reduced to seven, whist a report of 1779 noted five guns in the gun-platform casemates and three more on the platform in the outer court. By 1805 this had been increased again to six 24-pounders, six 12-pounders, and two 9-pounders. The castle improved as a residence after being granted in 1816 to the Reverend John Manning in 1816. His son Captain Charles Manning became the last governor of the Isle of Portland in 1834. A much larger new fort was built higher up in the 1850s to command the harbour then being improved with a new breakwater, but the castle returned to military use after Captain Manning's death in 1869 and remained thus until it became an ancient monument in state care in the 1950s.

Portland Castle

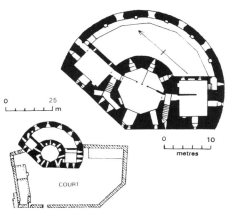

Plans of Portland Castle

The castle consists of a keep 15.5m in diameter with a fan-shaped gun platform placed on the seaward side of it. The platform has two levels, each with gunports for five cannon. The lower level was once roofed (see the roof-mark on the keep wall) but now forms an open court and the upper level has a wall-walk (added later) and a parapet which is curved on the outer face. Originally there was also a third tier of guns on the keep roof. On the north and SE the platform terminates in two storey wings of rooms opening off the keep and the flat faces of these wings continue along the side of the keep to meet at an obtuse angle. In the wings are a number off cross-loops. The north wing contains the captain's room over what was later used as a barrack room, each level having a latrine at the north end (the lower one has been altered), whilst the SE wing contains two bedrooms over a kitchen with an original fireplace (the oven is 19th century). The keep itself contains two octagonal halls with two rooms partitioned off in the east quadrant. The entrance is via a dog-leg passage into the lower hall. The doorway has a drawbar-slot and slits above for the chains of the drawbridge over the former moat. There is a connecting spiral stair on the south, although the stair to the roof is on the north.

The main building lies on the north side of a outer court 50m by 30m which is roughl rectangular but with the southern corner cut off. Over the gateway in the SW wall are the arms of Charles II. Three guns were once mounted on a platform in the east corner and another gun lay at the north corner. In the west corner is a building which was once the brew-house and stables, then later became the master gunner's house, subsequently was the residence of the commanding officer of the naval establishment H.M.S Osprey, and which is now the shop and tea-room.

POWERSTOCK CASTLE   SY 522959   F

King John acquired the manor in 1205 and by 1207 had spent £373 on building himself a hunting seat here. Vaults survived until the 18th century but the stone was later removed to supply a lime kiln. There are buried footings of a hall and chamber block on the north side of a platform 45m across with a rock-cut ditch on the other sides. There was also a curtain wall and other buildings. The platform lies on the north side (where there is a steep drop) of a circular bailey 150m across which itself lies within an Iron Age hilltop fort. The bailey shows evidence of the corework of a curtain wall probably set on a low cliff created artificially. This may be later, although the site was little used after King John's last visit in 1213 and his son Henry III in 1266 granted Powerstock to Sir Ralph de Gorges, who preferred his seat at Bradpole.

Buried remains of King John's hall block at Powerstock

Rufus Castle

RUFUS CASTLE   SY 697712   V

Set on an isolated rock high up on the SE side of Portland Bill is a mid 15th century pentagonal enclosure built by Richard, Duke of York. It measures about 12m across within walls 2m thick in which are segmental-headed upper embrasures containing single circular gunloops. The SE wall is thinner and is strengthened by two later buttresses. The entrance faces SW, but another entrance has been forced through the north wall, where there is a modern bridge over a roadway cut through the rock. At wall-walk level in the middle of the north and west sides are groups of three corbels for machicolations. These sides, which meet at a right angle which is chamfered off, appear to lie on older foundations. These may be a relic of the castle captured from King Stephen by Robert, Earl of Gloucester in 1142, or the building which Richard de Clare was licensed by Henry III to crenellate in 1258. The castle has no certain connection with William II, known as Rufus on account of his red hair, nor is it known how the castle acquired its other name of Bow and Arrow.

SANDSFOOT CASTLE   SY 675773   V

This was one of Henry VIII's artillery forts, begun in 1539 probably using stone from recently dissolved Bindon Abbey. Completed in 1540 at a cost of £3887, the fort commanded Portland Harbour, together with Portland Castle on the Isle of Portland. The remains are those of a two storey rectangular block 18m by 14m over walls 2.3m thick, much defaced externally but with some widely splayed upper gunloops of ashlar still remaining. The north end wall contains the entrance with a portcullis groove and a staircase and there is a fireplace and oven at the south end, where the sea has washed away a polygonal gun platform. A single storey gatehouse on the east side shown in an 18th century engraving has also vanished. In 1588 there was a garrison of 50 men here. The castle was de-garrisoned in 1665 although it remained in use as a store until the 1690s. From it has come the royal coat of arms over the south doorway of All Saints' Church at Wyke Regis. An outer rampart was added during the Civil War, when the castle vaults accommodated a mint.

Sandsfoot Castle

Sandsfoot Castle

SHAFTSBURY CASTLE   ST 857228   F

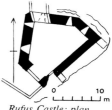

On a strong promontory site is a triangular ringwork. In 1949 a halfpenny of King Stephen was found in the "Cobbler's Pit" in the middle of the site. The town may have been fortified in connection with King Alfred's campaigns against the Danes but there are no remains of that era, not even of the famous Benedictine nunnery that Alfred founded there.

Rufus Castle: plan

Sandsfoot Castle

SHERBORNE CASTLE   ST 648168   E

This castle was built by Roger, Bishop of Sarum in the 1120s. Under Henry I he was Chancellor and then Justiciar and effectively ruled England when the king was away on trips to Normandy. The castle was seized by King Stephen in 1139 and was then retained as a royal castle, despite the continued claims upon it by later bishops. The building erected by Bishop Roger was so comfortable as a residence and so strong as a fortress that it did not require much modification in later years, although King John spent over £100 on general maintenance works. Repairs to roofs are recorded in the 1230s, whilst further work was done in 1299 and 1317. Edward III granted the castle to William Montague, Earl of Salisbury, but Bishop Robert Wyville pressed his claim to the castle again in 1354 and eventually got possession, although 2500 marks had to paid to the earl and 500 marks to the king to settle the matter.

After the Reformation the Crown managed to regain possession of the castle. Queen Elizabeth leased it in 1592 to Sir Walter Raleigh and he modified the old building before deciding to erect a new lodge (now also known as Sherborne Castle) beyond the lake to the south. In 1600 he added hexagonal turrets to this rectangular new lodge. Under James I Raleigh fell from favour and was eventually executed after years of imprisonment in the Tower of London, whilst Sherborne was granted to Sir John Digby in 1617. During the Civil War Lord Digby was one of the king's principal advisors and the old castle was garrisoned from 1642 and 1645. It was besieged by Fairfax for a fortnight in August 1645 before being taken by storm and subsequently dismantled. The Wingfield Digby family handed custody of the ruin over to the state in 1956 and it is now maintained by English Heritage. See pages 7 & 12.

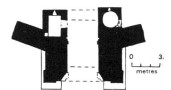

SW gateway plan

The SW gateway at Sherborne

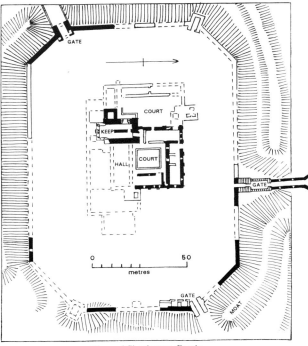

Plan of Sherborne Castle

The ringwork at Basing House

The 5th Marquess supported Charles I and his house at Basing withstood Parliamentary attacks in 1643. After the battle of Cheriton in 1644 Parliament tried to obtain Basing through treachery but this was foiled. After being closely besieged from May 1644 the house was finally taken by storm under Oliver Cromwell's personal supervision in November. Basing was regarded by Parliament as a bastion of Catholicism and their treatment of both the buildings and the garrison was very rough, whilst the marquess was sent to the Tower of London. After the Restoration the 6th Marquess, later created Duke of Bolton, demolished what remained of the buildings and landscaped the grounds to serve a new house built next to the great barn. This house in turn was later destroyed by fire and demolished by 1740 after which the family moved to a new house at Hackwood. The site has been in the custody of Hampshire County Council for preservation as a monument since 1972.

The site consists of a huge ringwork 80m in diameter, beyond the ditch of which is a 17th century outer rampart with bastions, a rectangular bailey 85m by 55m on the north, a large east bailey through the edge of which a canal was cut in the 1790s, and a walled garden occupying another outer bailey to the NW. The garden was restored to its supposed 17th century layout in 1989-90 and has a 16th century dovecote at the NW corner. Its brick surrounding walls have diaper decoration and have rough musketry loopholes made during the Civil War. South of the garden can be seen a 90m length of the complex sewerage system. The Bothey built nearby as a museum in 1908 contains part of an older building. The rectangular bailey contains the base of a gatehouse with four corner turrets on the west side but no evidence of a curtain wall. The east bailey contained the embattled "New House" built in the 1560s. This part bore the brunt of Cromwell's bombardment and attack, during which it was burnt, and little remains of it apart from a well. The house had two courts with three gatehouses. An excavation by Channel Four's Time Team found part of what is thought to have been the middle gateway, but they failed to find positive traces of the late 17th century house near the 36m long barn on the north side of the road skirting the site. On the south side of this road are remains of an outer gateway.

Basing House

Bishop's Waltham Palace

The ringwork contains the lower parts of the brick embattled house built in the 1530s. The rampart was faced with walls inside and out, creating a terrace about 10m wide. The outer wall has pilaster buttresses at intervals of about 12m. What stands now of the walls on the NW side may, at least in part, date from the landscaping of the 1690s, when the rampart was possibly heightened to provide elevated views of the grounds. So the complex of buildings inside may not have originally been quite as sheltered by ramparts as the remains are now. There were several private courts and a fan-shaped main court with a cobbled surface and a 15m deep well behind the huge north-facing gatehouse with four circular corner turrets, the outer two seemingly detached from the main building. Excavations have found traces of two earlier gatehouses in this position, one of them probably 13th century work. On the west side lay the hall, about 20m long by 10m wide, with a cellar below it. At the south end was an older medieval building of stone. West of the hall north end a hexagonal kitchen with three huge fireplaces is built into and against the outer rampart.

BISHOP'S WALTHAM PALACE   SU 553174   E

Waltham was one of several castles and defensible palaces erected by Henry de Blois, who became Bishop of Winchester in 1129. It may have been at least partly dismantled by Henry II in 1155, when the bishop, a brother of the previous king, Stephen, was in exile, and most of the existing buildings are thought to be of the 1160s and 70s. Henry II held court in the palace in 1182 when Richard of Ilchester was bishop, and his son Richard I used the palace similarly in 1194. Henry III was also a frequent visitor. William of Wykeham, bishop from 1367 to 1404, and an important minister under Edward III remodelled the 12th century apartments, the work being supervised by the noted architects William Wynford and Henry Yevele. In all Bishop Wykeham spent over £1300 upon the palace at Waltham and made it his principal residence in his old age. He was succeeded by Henry Beaufort, who lived until 1447 and added a top storey to the tower at the SW corner. A new chapel was under construction in 1416, but from 1417 to 1427 it remained incomplete, probably because Beaufort had to pay a huge fine to regain Henry V's favour after falling out with him. A new north range of lodgings was built in 1438-43 at a cost of £1000. Bishop Waynflete, who died at the palace in 1486, entertained Henry VI at Waltham in 1450, and Edward IV in 1476.

In 1551 Bishop Ponet surrendered the palace to Edward VI in return for an annual payment. It was then granted to Sir William Paulet, created Marquess of Winchester, and was visited by the boy king in 1552. In 1554 Queen Mary occupied the palace when awaiting the arrival of Philip II of Spain, after which they were married at Winchester. Shortly before her death in 1558 Mary restored the palace to the bishop. During the Civil War the palace was surrendered to Parliament after the Royalist defeat at Cheriton and was probably burnt. The stonework may have survived, only to be removed later by the bishops and others. Some parts remained in use for a survey of 1806 records a farmhouse, barn, stable, cowhouse and cartlodge. The site was sold into private hands in 1889 but Viscount Cunningham placed the ruin in state guardianship in 1952. It is now in the care of English Heritage.

Chapel remains at Bishop's Waltham Palace

Bishop's Waltham Palace

A moat, still water filled on the north side, surrounds the rectangular platform 140m long by up to 90m wide which formed the main court, now divided in two by a low 17th century wall. Only footings remains of the 15th century north range except for the easternmost end, which remained in use as a farmhouse and now houses the custodian's office and exhibitions. This range contained lodgings with fireplaces in stacks facing the moat, and a two storey timber-framed arcade facing the main court. Not much more remains of the gatehouse at the NW corner, a rectangular 14th century building remodelled in the 15th century. The north end of the east side is filled by a late 14th century range containing lodgings over bakehouses. Further south are foundations of a 15th century chapel. Adjoining the west end is the apse of the original chapel of the 1130s, or rather its crypt.

The bishop's audience chamber lay in the western half of the south range, but the remodelled upper parts of the 1390s have gone, except for a short length on the south, leaving just the 12th century lower walls. The lines of the steep 12th century roof and its much flatter 14th century successor can be seen on the east face of the 9.5m square tower at the SW corner. The tower contained two private rooms for the bishop over a dark basement reached from above, the walls being of the 1160s or 70s but the features late 14th century. The third storey room has a latrine. The pilaster buttress clasping the outer corner does not continue into the fourth storey, which was an early 15th century addition. The upper rooms were reached by a spiral stair in a turret on the NE corner, most of which has fallen. A narrow 14th century block connects this tower to the state rooms further north but there was a 12th century room here for a window from it survives partly in the outer wall. The original main public hall of the 1160s or 70s measuring 22m by 9m was probably at courtyard level. A section of wall arcading survives in the north end of the west wall. In the remodelling of 1379-81 the hall was placed at a higher level and given a new north wall and five fine windows of two lights with transoms in the outer west wall. The inner wall is destroyed to its footings. East of here Bishop Beaufort created a cloister in the early 15th century. The north part of the range was rebuilt in 1387-93 and then contained chambers over service rooms with a lofty kitchen beyond.

In the 1490s Bishop Langton enclosed a garden 180m by 150m to he south and east by a brick wall, which then extended along the east side to enclose an outer court with a gateway facing the town. The SE corner is missing but the SW and NE corners of the garden still have two storey octagonal pavilions. A series of wide lakes lay to the west and the bishop's park lay to the south beyond the garden.

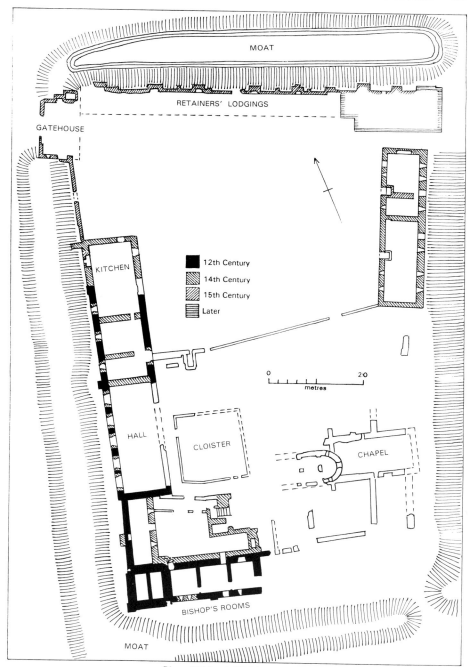

MOAT

RETAINERS' LODGINGS

GATEHOUSE

KITCHEN

12th Century
14th Century
15th Century
Later

HALL

CLOISTER

CHAPEL

0   20
metres

BISHOP'S ROOMS

MOAT

Plan of Bishop's Waltham Palace

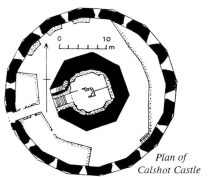

Bitterne Palace

Calshot Castle

*Plan of
Calshot Castle*

BITTERNE PALACE   SU 433133

Some medieval walling with one 13th century lancet remains of a house of the bishops of Winchester which included a substantial tower. It lay within what remained of the defensive wall and ditch of the Roman port of Clausentum, on a promontory on the east bank of the River Itchen, 3km inland from the open sea. The building was remodelled in the 19th century and then made into flats in the 1950s after being damaged by wartime bombing.

BLENDWORTH CASTLE   SU 725122

In woodland between Blendworth and Rowland's Castle is a ringwork with a barbican on one side and a bailey. A second earthwork to the SW could be a siegework.

BRADLEY RINGWORK   SU 645413

On the edge of a wood 1km SE of Bradley are traces of a possible unfinished ringwork.

Calshot Castle

CALSHOT CASTLE   SU 488025   E

This artillery fort on a spit at the entrance of Southampton Water was begun by Henry VIII in 1539 and mostly completed by the end of 1540, when there was a garrison of a captain, a deputy, eight gunners and five soldiers. Materials came from the newly dissolved monasteries and lead for the roof is known to have come from Beaulieu Abbey. The castle had 36 guns, although by 1559 there were only ten that were serviceable left within it. The castle was refitted in 1584 after the keep was gutted by fire. It does not seem to have seen action in the Civil War. In 1725 the castle was armed with 13 6-pounder guns although only shortly before there had been 25 guns. In a drastic remodelling of the castle in the 1770s the outer wall was lowered, the gatehouse rebuilt and the keep given a new roof and parapet. After the Napoleonic Wars the castle was used as a coastguard base. In the 1890s a battery of the new 4.7inch quick-firing guns was built immediately to the south, and in 1907 two 12-pounder guns were installed on the keep roof. A naval seaplane base was established alongside the castle in 1913. After the Second World War the castle reverted to being a coastguard base but eventually the coastguards were provided with a new tower and the castle became an ancient monument in state care.

The castle consists of a three storey central keep 15m in diameter and 12m high closely surrounded by a gun-platform with an external diameter of 36m, itself surrounded by a wet moat 9m wide and 2.5m deep. The keep is octagonal internally and externally lower down but the outside is circular high up. The outer wall of the gun platform has 16 sides internally and externally below the mounding marking the top of the battered plinth. The outer wall has 15 gunports, now forming embrasures in a parapet, although originally the gunports were arched over and there was a parapet at a higher level. Two gunports survive in their original form on either side of the gatehouse, which was later extended to incorporate them. Over the entrance, which has a portcullis groove, is a panel for former royal arms and two dumb-bell shaped gunloops. In the 1890s a searchlight battery was installed in the eastern part of the gun-platform. The electric generators for the lights were installed in the keep basement, which was given a new entrance and a thick concrete ceiling in place of the original stone vault. The basement was originally reached by a blocked doorway off the stair from the court to the main room above. The upper rooms have also suffered considerable alteration and the top is all 18th and 20th century work but the third storey room retains two blocked original fireplaces and a latrine on the SE side.

CRONDALL: BARLEY POUND   SU 797468

The oval ringwork 60m by 50m with two baileys to the south of it and a weaker outer bailey to the NW probably represents the Bishop of Winchester's castle of Lidelea captured by King Stephen in 1147. The now-destroyed mound at Bentley (794463) and the motte known as Powderham Castle at 803469, near the hospital to the east were presumably siegeworks. The latter may have seen further use and has a counterscarp bank to the ditch and traces of possible walling on the summit.

GODSHILL: CASTLE HILL   SU 166162   F

On a wooded promontory above the east side of the River Avon are traces of a ringwork and outer enclosures. It may have been built in 1148 by supporters of the Empress Matilda during their attempt to capture the Bishop of Winchester's castle at Downton in Wiltshire 5km to the north.

HASILWORTH CASTLE   SZ 607975

On the shore not far SW of the 18th century Fort Monckton lay one of Henry VIII's artillery forts, built in 1545-6.

HURST CASTLE   SZ 318897   E

Construction of an artillery fort here was first mooted in 1539 by commissioners appointed by Henry VIII, and construction began early in 1541. A garrison was installed under Thomas Bertie in 1542, although building work continued until 1544. A survey of 1547 mentions twenty guns at Hurst, although by 1559 there were only ten, and there was then a garrison consisting of a captain, a deputy, a porter, a master gunner, eleven gunners and nine soldiers. In 1628 the garrison were unable to stop some Flemish ships passing by since no powder or shot were available and only a few of the 27 guns were usable. The castle held a Parliamentary garrison throughout the Civil War and in December 1648 Charles I was held prisoner within it before being taken to London for trial and execution. The castle was later used as a prison for Catholics, one priest being held here from 1700 until his death in 1729.

Hurst Castle

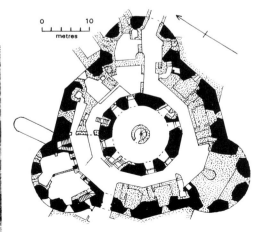

0   10
metres

Plan of Hurst Castle

Hurst Castle

When war with France broke out in the 1790s the castle required considerable repair and re-arming, being given 18 9-pounder guns, whilst a pair of five gun batteries armed with captured French 36-pounder guns, were established alongside it. In 1803-6 the central tower was remodelled to carry 6 24-pounder guns on the roof, new vaults being inserted over the basement and topmost storey. New earth and shingle batteries beside the castle were built in the 1850s, when the south bastion and adjacent curtain walls were also remodelled to provide casemates for heavy guns. The new outside batteries were soon regarded as too exposed to withstand heavy shellfire and between 1861 and 1870 they were replaced by massive new structures of stone and concrete. Shells for the new batteries of 12.5" and 10" guns were stored in the basement of the old keep. New quick-firing guns were added to the armaments in the 1890s. The castle was garrisoned during both World Wars although the original 16th century building been opened as an ancient monument back in 1933. The rest of the site was opened to the public in the 1950s.

The original castle lies at the centre of the 19th century complex, with a 220m long wing extending to the west and wider but shorter wing extending to the NE. The old part consisted of a three storey twelve-sided central keep 20m in diameter and 12m high surrounded by a gun-platform which would also be twelve sided but for the fact that externally alternate pairs of sides are replaced by semi-circular bastions 20m in diameter. Originally there were gunports in each side of the outer wall between the bastions and four in each bastion but the only original ones still open are two in the NW bastion. Immediately south of this bastion lies the entrance, which has a portcullis groove. Originally there was also a moat outside. There was another tier of embrasures in the parapets above, those of the bastions being slightly higher than those of walls in between. The bastions were later remodelled to contain pairs of rooms, but those in the south bastion, and also the casemates created on either side in the 1850s, were filled up solid with shingle and concrete in the 1880s. The circular interior of the keep has seen much alteration in the 19th century. The entrance into the middle storey has the date 1585 over it. The paired window embrasures here are original, and a latrine opens off one to the SE, although the windows themselves are early 19th century. The keep always had a central spiral stair (shown in old prints as capped with a ribbed dome with a central finial) but the existing stair only leads down to the magazine below and direct to the roof. Thus the top storey is now reached by an external stair on the NW side. This room was originally subdivided and has four fireplaces and several window embrasures. Doorways once led from this upper room to timber bridges to the tops of the bastions.

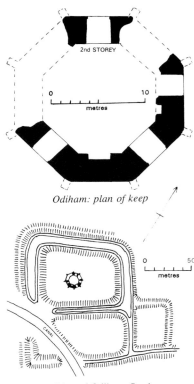

Odiham: plan of keep

Plan of Odiham Castle

Merdon Castle

LONG SUTTON CASTLE   SU 757461

There are traces of a ringwork with evidence of a building of uncertain date and purpose.

MERDON CASTLE   SU 421265

This castle is thought to have been built in the 1130s by Henry de Blois, Bishop of Winchester, and to have been at least partly dismantled by Henry II in 1156. A tower is mentioned in 1286 and 13th and 14th century documents also mention a hall, a chamber over an undercroft, a kitchen, larder and a middle gateway. The ringwork stands up to 13m high on the north, although the rampart is missing on the south, towards the bailey. They both lie within an Iron Age rampart and ditch. On the north side are ruins of a building 10m wide by at least 12m long over walls up to 2.2m thick. There is a longitudinal crosswall and the westernmost part has an archway through the north wall. This building, which stands in a defaced and overgrown state to a height of about 12m, has been described as a gatehouse, but since it faces a steep drop down the ringwork bank any entrance it contained can only have been a minor postern. It is more likely that the building was a solar tower with a hall block adjoining it.

NETLEY CASTLE   SU 451088   V

After Henry VIII's death in 1547, it was acknowledged that William Paulet, Lord St John, had built this fort on the east shore of Southampton Water a few years earlier at the late king's request, and William was allowed to provide it with cannon and a garrison, with a grant of lands to defray his expenses. The castle formed a rectangular block, with gun batteries at either end of a low central tower. Two barbicans or small enclosures are also mentioned in 1547. The building was adapted as a residence in the 1620s but remained little altered apart from an oriel being added in the seaward side until in 1857 it was heightened and given a Gothic tower. The crenels of the parapet, which was rounded towards the field, were used to locate the new upper windows. A dining room was then added at the NW end and further additions on the landward side were made in 1885-90, although the original entrance there still survives. The tower of 1857 was then remodelled and given a stair turret.

Odiham Castle

Netley Castle

ODIHAM CASTLE   SU 725519   F

This ruin lies on flat ground on the east bank of the River Whitewater near where it is crossed by the Basingstoke Canal, 3.2km NW of Odiham church. Access to the site is from the canal towpath. King John spent over £1000 on constructing it between 1207 and 1212 and was a frequent visitor. It was captured in 1216 by Prince Louis of France after a desperate defence made by a garrison of just thirteen men, but was recaptured in 1217 for the young Henry III by William Marshall. In later years Odiham was often held in dower by queen consorts. Edward I held a parliament here in 1303, and the castle was fortified by Edward II in 1307. Robert Lewer attacked the castle for Thomas of Lancaster in 1321. He was beaten off but the defences may have been damaged since considerable repairs were executed in 1324-5. David Bruce, King of Scots was held captive in the castle by Edward III until in 1357 he was released for a ransom of 100,000 marks. In 1386 Richard II had the castle fortified against the Duke of Gloucester. It seems to have been ruinous by the early 16th century.

The castle had an octagonal keep lying within one of a pair of moated rectangular platforms plus outworks. One platform is now bisected by the canal. The other platform around the keep measures 75m by 45m and must have been walled in stone with a gatehouse and possibly corner towers. The 14th century accounts mention a bridge on the west side and gates facing west, east and south. The keep is 18m in diameter over walls up to 3m thick and although most of the Caen stone facing has been robbed the flint corework stands over 13m high. There were buttresses on the outer corners. The keep contained two upper storeys of rooms with fireplaces and windows probably of two lights over a basement with narrow loops. No stairs or latrines remain. It appears that the floor beams radiated from a central post.

PORTCHESTER CASTLE   SU 624046   E

The Roman fort of Portus Adurni begun probably shortly after 285, when Carausius was appointed by the Emperor Diocletian to clear the English Channel of barbarian raiders, remained defensible throughout the medieval period and is still surprising complete even today. The fort continued to be occupied in some fashion, even if only by farmers until the 9th century. After the fort was acquired by King Edward the Elder in exchange for Bishop's Waltham in 904 it was repaired and garrisoned as a burh against Viking raids. Excavations found evidence of a large aisled hall of this era with a courtyard containing a well and a latrine block. The buildings were later remodelled and a square stone tower added c1000, whilst the Watergate was rebuilt in stone re-using Roman materials.

There is no mention of a castle at Portchester in Domesday Book of 1086 but it is thought that the then owner, William Mauduit, had rebuilt the Landgate and closed off the NW corner of the fort with a palisade and ditch by the time of his death c1100. His son Robert was drowned along with Henry I's only legitimate son William in the White Ship disaster of 1120. Porchester then reverted to Henry I and it was probably then that the keep straddling the NW corner of the fort was begun, whilst the curtain wall of the bailey is not much later. By about 1130 the castle had been acquired by William Pont de l'Arche, who married the Mauduit heiress. The keep was almost doubled in height either by this lord shortly before his death in the late 1140s or by the Mauduits, who regained the castle for a few years before it again reverted to Henry II. No work on the castle is then recorded until it was garrisoned during the rebellion of 1173 and used as a prison for the earl and countess of Leicester. In the next few years the domestic buildings against the curtain walls were rebuilt in stone.

Gateway passage at Porchester

Keep at Porchester

Porchester Castle

King John was a frequent visitor to Porchester and here learned of Normandy being lost to the French king Philip Augustus in 1204. The chamber and wardrobe built in 1211 may have been adjacent to the keep forebuilding. During the rebellion against John in 1215 Porchester was captured by Prince Louis of France. In 1217 the regents for the young Henry III ordered the castle to be demolished but this was not acted upon. The expenditure recorded in 1229-30 may have been the building of the east range, whilst a barbican is thought to have been built in 1256. The domestic buildings were described as old and ruinous in 1275 but the gates were repaired in 1296, when there was a danger of a French attack. From 1273 until 1330 the castle was held in dower by various queen consorts. During the 1320s about £1100 was spent by Edward II on providing the three gateways with new portcullises, remodelling the keep forebuilding and updating the royal apartments around the west and south sides of the courtyard. The ditch and rampart NW of the castle isolating the promontory on which it stands are also probably of this period. A report of 1335 mentions the castle as containing 100 crossbows, most of them in decay, 300 bolts for them, and nearly 1000 arrows, although the ten longbows were described as useless. French raids on Southampton and Portsmouth in 1338 instigated repairs at Porchester. Stock of munitions were brought it and a garrison of 10 men-at-arms and 40 bowmen was installed. In 1436 Edward III here assembled the army which he was to lead into victory at Crecy. The hall was rebuilt in 1356 and the chamber between it and keep remodelled. Work carried out in 1362 included re-leading the keep roof and making a new chapel.

The tower in the NE corner of the bailey is named after Sir Rodert de Ashton, who became the keeper of the castle in 1376. The tower is first mentioned in 1385, when it was completed by his successor Robert Bardolf. Handguns are first mentioned at Portchester in this period, and the tower top storey contains ports for firing them out of. About the same time the outer part of the barbican was added. Richard II's marriage to Isabella of France in 1396 seems to have instigated another building campaign at Porchester, where the royal apartments were again rebuilt, vaults were added inside the keep, the Landgate was rebuilt and the Watergate was re-roofed.

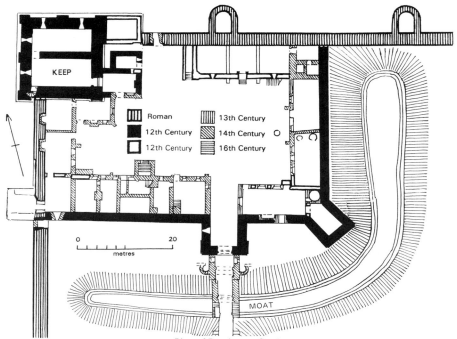

Plan of Porchester Castle

In 1415 Henry V departed from Porchester on the campaign which led to the victory at Agincourt. The castle was reported to be in decay in 1441 and 1450 but minor repairs were carried out by Henry VII and it must have been habitable at the time of Henry VIII's visit in 1535. In the 1540s it was superseded by his new series of artillery forts and by 1563 served only as a military hospital. A storehouse built in the outer ward in the 1520s seems to have been removed to Portsmouth by the 1580s. Sir Thomas Cornwallis entertained Queen Elizabeth at the castle in 1601. He added an upper storey to the east range and inserted other windows elsewhere. In 1632 Charles I sold off the then redundant castle to Sir William Uvedale. A force of 4000 dragoons of the Parliamentary army was quartered in the castle in 1644. Prisoners taken during the Dutch War of 1665-7 were kept in the keep, and the castle was again used as a prison from 1702 during the War of the Spanish Succession. More Spanish prisoners were kept at Porchester in the 1740s during the War of the Austrian Succession. By 1745 2000 prisoners were crowded into the bailey buildings and keep, although they were allowed to exercise in a specially-built yard in the outer bailey. In the 1750s Edward Gibbon, later noted for his Roman studies, commanded a garrison of 234 men supervising 3200 prisoners from the Seven Years War.

The castle was again used as a prison during the Napoleonic wars, and by 1810 it contained about 7000 prisoners. Barrack blocks both for prisoners and guards were built in the outer bailey and extra floors were inserted in the keep, whilst the basement was converted into a theatre to help keep the inmates amused. After 1814 the prisoners were replaced by injured soldiers from Wellington's army, and imprisoned deserters. In 1810 the castle was returned to William Uvedale's descendants the Thistlethwaites, but soon became ruinous. It was placed in state guardianship in 1926 and is now maintained by English Heritage.

The Roman fort forming the outer bailey measures about 180m square. The walls were originally 3m thick but except in the NW quarter robbing of materials from the inner face for use elsewhere has reduced the wall to about half that thickness and the wall-walk and parapet are 14th century, although not different in appearance from what they would have looked like originally. The parapet reaches to 8m above the level berm between the wall and the ditch beyond it. The wall was flanked by twenty U-shaped hollow bastions 6m wide projecting 6m from the wall and rising slightly above it, those at the corners being set diagonally. The keep has replaced that at the NW and the sea has washed away that at the SE. On the south side the full set of four intermediate bastions still remain, but on the west and north sides one has been lost, and on the east side only two now remain.

Inner gateway at Porchester

The Roman fort had postern passages in the middle of the north and south walls, a Watergate on the east towards the sea and the main entrance or Landgate on the west. The main gates originally had small courts in front of gatehouses recessed within the walls. The existing Watergate occupying the south part of the wide Roman gateway is partly late Saxon (see the inner arch). It was remodelled in the 1320s and after storm damage the diagonally buttressed outer part with a portcullis was added in 1335. The Landgate is early Norman and lies upon the northern part of its Roman counterpart. Excavations found evidence of a Saxon timber structure in front of it. The outer arch was replaced in the 1320s but the two upper storeys reached by a stair in the thick north wall are mostly of the 1390s. There was then a barbican in front of it.

Keep section

In the SE corner of the fort is a parish church which served an Augustinian priory founded in 1133. The cruciform church with a central tower has lost its south transept and the three east apses of the chancel and transepts. The canons found living in a fortress inconvenient and by 1150 had transferred to Southwick. The claustral buildings south of the church were left incomplete but the latrine drains of the reredorter at the south end of the dormitory can be seen on the outer wall. Excavations have found traces of medieval buildings on either side of the Watergate and an 11th century timber hall west of the priory church, whilst the buried footings of a 16th century barn 12m wide extend for 75m northwards from the south wall. As many as nine barrack blocks stood in the outer bailey at the end of the Napoleonic Wars.

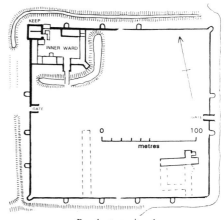

Porchester: site plan

In the 1120s or 30s an ashlar-faced wall 1.9m thick was built to close off the NW corner of the fort to form an inner bailey 58m by 37m. The wall is fronted by a wet moat and is flanked by a trapezoidal SE corner bastion up to 8m wide projecting diagonally and a gatehouse 9.6m wide on the south side. The keep at the NW corner and two Roman bastions flanked the other sides, although the bastion on the west has since collapsed. In the 1320s a vaulted porch or barbican was built in front of the gateway, which has wide clasping pilaster buttresses on its outer corners. The tiny round turrets on either side formed part of a low mantlet wall on the inner edge of the moat. The barbican was doubled in length in the 1380s with a new outer entrance with a portcullis, and in the 17th century it was extended again, with a tiny porter's lodge in the wall thickness on the west side. The courtyard has buildings of two storeys on all sides and there is a well close to the east range. The building east of the gateway is late 12th century and may have formed a chamber for knights, but by the 14th century it had become a workshop and in the 1490s it became a kitchen with an oven inserted at the east end. The east range was built in the 13th century to contain a kitchen with a stable or store north of it. It was remodelled in the 14th century and given an upper storey with three-light windows in the early 17th century. The lower level has now been re-roofed to provide a custodian's office.

The late 14th century Ashton's Tower fills the corner between the north and east ranges. It measures 10m by 8m and does not project beyond the curtain walls. The third storey has doorways to the curtain wall-walks and one east facing keyhole-gunport. Another faces south on the fourth storey and it seems that originally there was one on each side at that level. The late 12th century north range formed the constable's house and contained a hall and chamber over a vaulted basement. A stair at the west end led to the curtain wall-walk and the upper rooms, remodelled in the 14th century and now very ruined. Of the 1390s is the room built on top of the Roman bastion here, with a latrine set over a heavy squinch arch on the east side.

The ranges on the west and south sides of the court formed the royal apartments. Although they contain some early and mid 14th century work, they are substantially of the 1390s and were embattled with roofs of nearly flat pitch containing louvres for the central fireplaces of the kitchen and great hall. There are keyhole-shaped gunports in the sections of parapet remaining on the west range. Next to the gateway was a lofty kitchen, from which steps led up to a service area between it and the hall, which was set over storerooms at the east end and two chambers at the west end, and was a fine apartment 16m long reached from the court by a vaulted porch

The west gateway (Landgate) at Porchester

on the north side. However, since its four tall two-light windows with transoms faced north, the hall must have been rather dark. A spiral stair by the porch led to a chamber over it and to a larger chamber over the service area east of the hall. A passage at the hall NW corner then led to the great chamber on the upper floor of the west range. From here there was access to a room extending along the south side of the keep and the king's own room tucked into the SW corner, with one south facing window pierced through the older curtain. Under these chambers are rooms with a few older features used by household officials. The lower room on the north side against the keep was the Exchequer Chamber, used as an office by the household officials.

East Gate at Porchester

The keep at the NW corner measures about 17m square over walls 2.5m thick reducing to 2m at second storey level and 1.8m higher up. At one time the building was only about 16m high to the wall-walks and contained just a hall with a chamber to the north, beyond a cross-wall, with cellars below dimly lit by double-splayed loops. There is evidence to suggest that the keep was built up over a single storey building, onto the walls of which the ashlar outer facing and splayed plinth were grafted. The cellar were covered with ribbed vaults in the 1390s. What later become the low third storey when the building was heightened by another 11m in the mid 12th century was originally a roof-space, each compartment being covered by a roof with a central gulley. Small loops of uncertain purpose were tucked under these roofs. The corner and mid-wall pilaster buttresses are not continued up in the extension. The chamber fireplace backs onto the north mid-wall pilaster, and the NE corner contains a latrine reached from the chamber, whilst a long passage from the hall extended to another latrine in the NW corner.

The SW corner contains a spiral stair connecting all the levels except the fourth storey, and the SE corner contains a well. The extra levels inserted to accommodate French prisoners are connected by timber staircases within the rooms. The chamber windows, enlarged in the 14th century, face north and consequently this room was always rather dark. The upper rooms have rectangular windows, those in the east and south walls of the fifth storey being of two lights recessed under a round head. The northern room here has a latrine. The parapets were part of a slight heightening in the late 14th century and the low-pitched roof is a modern replacement of that then provided. On the east and west sides the parapet slopes up in the middle.

The keep entrance doorway at the NE corner of its hall is reached by an L-shaped flight of steps up between a forebuilding and the Roman fort wall, although this was probably not the original arrangement since the forebuilding was rebuilt several times. The room south of this stair formed a prison. Above the southern part of the forebuilding was a chapel, but little of it remains other than a round arch within the keep east wall. In the 1320s chambers were built beyond this corner, only to be removed in the 1390s. The block north of the entrance stair was added in the late 12th century and projects out across the line of the former Roman wall. The upper oriel facing north here is late 15th century, evidence that this was once a chamber of some importance.

PORTSDOWN CASTLE   SU 639073   V

The main road leading down off the Portsdown ridge towards Southwick cuts across the west part of the outworks of a low motte within a square bailey, although quarrying for chalk has mutilated all the earthworks.

PORTSMOUTH TOWN DEFENCES   SZ 629994   V

Richard I is said to have built a wall to protect his naval dockyard at Portsmouth, and his house at Kingshall Green was protected by a ditch, but Richard II clearly found the town in need of better protection and created a new rampart, palisade and ditch on the landward side. Although it looks like one of Henry VIII's blockhouses, and has evidence of eight seaward-facing gunports of his period in the lowest lowel, the Round Tower is thought to have been originally built by Henry V. It was connected by a chain to a vanished tower at SZ 626993 on the Gosport side of the harbour. The two upper levels may be late 17th century when the adjacent Eighteen Gun Battery was built, but were remodelled c1800-14 and the walls thickened internally, whilst the top is of 1847-50. The Square Tower beyond the King James' Gate of 1687 not far to the SE was built by Henry VII in 1490s, when the port was provided with a timber-framed dry-dock. The tower became the governor's residence but was was later cut down to form a magazine and in 1827 was refaced externally, whilst the interior was remodelled in 1847-50, buying most of the medieval work.

In the 1540s Henry VIII built a new gateway called the Lanport on the NE side of the town, having obscured a medieval gateway by building a large new bastion in front of it. Queen Elizabeth in the late 1560s added a bastion in the middle of the SE side and replaced the round corner bastions by others of the improved arrow-head shape. The moat was also widened and the quay on the NW side of the town was cut off by a new stone wall. By Charles II's reign Portsmouth was England's premier naval base, and, under the supervision of Sir Bernard de Gomme, the defences were repaired and improved by outworks including ravelins and a glacis. All that survives of these works following demolition in the 1870s is the rampart running from the Saluting Platform SE of the Square Tower to the King's Bastion at the south corner.

Round Tower at Portsmouth

ROWLAND'S CASTLE   SU 733105

West of the railway is a 10m high motte with traces of possible masonry and two overgrown baileys.

ST ANDREWS POINT CASTLE   SZ 484059

Only slight traces remain of the moats of an artillery fort built by Henry VIII on the headland between the Hamble and Southampton Water. First mentioned in 1544, it had a square keep which was cracked by 1623. The courtyard seems to have been rectangular. A survey of 1593 also mentions a round tower.

SILCHESTER RINGWORK   SU 646625   E

Excavations have removed every trace of a ringwork which was built over the Roman amphitheatre in the early 12th century, probably by the Bluet family. Traces were found of a hall inside.

SOUTHAMPTON CASTLE SU 418114

The town was important port by the end of the 11th century, and since there is no evidence of major expenditure by Henry II on the royal castle which is first mentioned in 1153, it is likely that Henry I had already provided the bailey with stone walls. The castle was captured by Prince Louis of France in 1216 but recaptured by William Marshall for the young Henry III in 1217. The building was still in use in 1599 when it contained 60 artillery pieces and had a garrison of 100 men but it was sold by James I and in 1650 stone was taken from the castle to repair the town walls.

The bailey was D-shaped with a 110m long straight west wall which survives as part of the circuit of town defences. This part is buttressed towards the south end, where there is a storeroom for goods landed on the quay outside, the vault of which originally had ribs. South of it is the Watergate, with remains of a deeply recessed 14th century gateway, now blocked. Between here and the south corner

Bar Gate at Southampton

lay the hall, set over another undercroft and having a latrine in a SE corner turret. In the late 14th century keyhole-shaped gunports were inserted in the outer wall here. At the NW corner of the bailey is a flat Norman buttress. On the NE a long section of 5m high walling with arcading ends with the footings of a twin round-towered gatehouse facing Castle Way. Originally the wall was higher and the arches were buried in a bank. A second gateway on the south side is thought to have been a rectangular tower with a barbican in front entered on the west side, an unusual arrangement since it entailed a right-angle turn difficult for horse-drawn carts. The vanished motte, probably of 11th century origin, was provided with a new shell keep with flanking round towers during the minority of Richard II. The keep seems to have been encircled by a mantlet or chemise wall, creating a citadel which John Leland in the 1540s described as "large, fair and very strong, both by worke and the site of it". It was ruinous by James I's reign and in 1804 the remains were incorporated in a huge gothick structure erected by the Marquis of Lansdowne. This was removed as early as 1818 and the motte lowered. Castle House of 1963 now stands on the site.

Castle bailey gateway at Southampton

God's House Gate on town walls

Bar Gate at Southampton

Southampton has one of the most impressive circuits of medieval town walls remaining in southern England. Only the walls of Canterbury, Chichester and Exeter are anywhere near as complete. The walls enclose a rectangle 680m long from north to south by 300m wide with the SW corner chamfered off. The landward facing east and north sides were protected by a double ditch and the castle lay towards the north end of the west side, and the NW corner may have originally formed an outer bailey. The southern part of the east wall is thought to be early 13th century. Most of the rest of the east and north sides seem to have been stone walled by the end of the 13th century although archaeological evidence suggests that the section south of the Polymond Tower at the NE corner was not built until the 14th century. The town was devastated by a French raid in 1338 since it was then still open to seaward. The openings between houses facing the quay were blocked in the 1360s, although the seaward defences were probably not completed until the 1380s.

The Bargate in the middle of the north side has a Late Norman inner arch of three chamfered orders. There are arrowloops in each of the two storeys of the D-shaped towers added on either side in the 1280s. The inner facade with four upper windows may also be of that period, although much restored in 1864. Between the central windows is a statue of George III, placed here in 1809 to take the place of an effigy of Queen Anne now on show in the museum inside the building. A rectangular outer part, largely masking the two drum towers was added c1400 and the upper room then became a guildhall reached by a long flight of steps on the east. The outer archway is flanked by buttresses rising up to the machicolated parapet. Over the archway is a row of five painted 18th century shields. Since 1932-7 the Bargate has been isolated in the middle of a traffic roundabout and the wall further west was breached in 1960 for a ring-road. At the NW corner is the circular Arundel Tower, named after a late 14th century governor of the castle, by whom it was heightened. The lowest of the upper stages is seven sided internally with a doorway facing west to a former salient now reduced to just a buttress, and three loops facing the field. The late 14th century wall from here to the Catchcold Tower is built against a cliff, so it is quite low internally, yet impressive outside. The Catchcold Tower is semi-circular, with a boldly corbelled parapet, and is a 15th century addition. The top room is vaulted and contains three gunports. The Forty Steps added against the outside of the wall beyond are of 1850. The wall then turns SW to meet the castle bailey.

Council housing now lies on the side of a salient between the castle SW corner and site of a minor gateway at the end of Simnel Street. South of here the wall takes the dramatic form of an arcade carrying the parapet over a series of buttresses built in front of the older walls of the merchants houses here, the seaward openings in which were blocked up. A postern lies in one of the recesses, in the arches of which were machicolations. South of here the late 12th century King John's House is one of the houses incorporated in the town wall. In the blocking of its openings are two early gunports. Beyond are the small rectangular Nicholls Tower and then the West Gate, which gave access to the town quay. Dating from the mid 14th century, it is a rectangular structure with a pointed tunnel vault over the passage, which was closed by two portcullises. The upper rooms have 16th century gunports. The so-called guard room adjoining to the south is more likely to have been a 17th century merchant's store. The wall beyond is arcaded, although it was not built against older houses, and in any case the first three arches are only of 1899. Little remains of the wall between the site of the Bugle Tower and the Water Gate, two other towers having vanished and only the base remaining of a third.

The Watergate retains one three storey circular tower adjoining a rectangular tower with a recessed south front with machicolations between buttresses, one of which contains latrines on each level. The basement was originally vaulted. The wall them swung southwards to the Watchbell Tower and then east to the early 14th century God's House Gate at the SE corner. The outermost of the two portcullis grooves in the vaulted passage is the result of 14th century remodelling of an older structure. Adjoining the gateway a building runs out eastward to connect with the three storey God's House Tower built c1400-20 to control the sluice of the east ditch. This impressive group of buildings now forms a museum. North of here is a well preserved section of the east wall complete with the wall-walk and parapet, leading to a semicircular tower with arrow loops. A more ruinous section beyond a gap has two shallowly projecting rectangular turrets. There is then quite a long gap before a very ruined section south of the site of the East Gate which had a Late Norman arch until it was demolished in 1775. Not far beyond is the Polymond Tower,

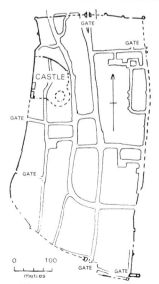

a circular structure at the NE corner, enlarged in the late 14th century. The topmost of three storeys was removed in 1828. The section from here back to the Bar Gate contains two semi-circular towers.

Plan of Southampton walls   *Southampton walls*

SOUTHSEA CASTLE   SZ 643980   O

This artillery fort of 1544 commands the eastern approach to Portsmouth. It failed to prevent the French entering the harbour the following year. The fort consisted of a square tower set within a square enclosure set at 45 degrees to the inner building and having rectangular gun platforms facing east and west. It lay gutted and empty for ten years after being accidentally burnt in 1626. Another fire caused some damage in 1640. The fort was captured by Parliamentary forces in 1642 and subsequently used as a prison. The defences were improved by the engineer De Gomme in 1683, with an outer glacis and a covered way. The east wing was wrecked by an explosion thought to have been caused by a kitchen fire setting off gunpowder. The building was remodelled internally c1790-1800 and partly rebuilt in 1814-16. It was used as a military prison for offenders from the Portsmouth Garrison in the 1840s and then in 1850 became the centre of a large new fortress. The fort remained in service throughout the two world wars. In 1960 it was acquired by Portsmouth Corporation and restored to its 1850 condition as a military museum.

The windows and the parapets of the central keep are late 19th century but original gunports facing south, east and west remain at second storey level. They were blocked in the 1680s but one facing south has been re-opened. Before the remodelling of c1790 the keep contained two small buildings facing across a central court. It now has a fine brick upper vault to support heavy guns on the roof. The surrounding enceinte was mostly refaced in 1814 and the south side was heightened in 1850. The south angle was rounded off in 1814 and new outer walls built on the north with buildings against them. Other buildings were erected within the enceinte and a covered walkway with musketry loops was built on the far side of the moat, with a passage linking it to the keep basement. A lighthouse painted in black and white was erected on the north side of the west gun platform in 1828. See p11.

SOUTHWICK CASTLE   SU 634092

In Place Wood, north of HMS Dryad, are the unimpressive remains of a ringwork with a bailey extending to the SW.

West Gate, Southampton town walls

Arcading on Southampton town walls

Southsea Castle

TITCHFIELD ABBEY   SU 542067   E

Thomas Wriothesley, one of Henry VIII's agents for the dissolution of the monasteries, obtained the former Premonstratensian abbey of Titchfield on its closure in December 1537. It was quickly converted into a semi-fortified house called Place House and in 1542 a pardon was obtained from the king for embattling the building without permission. The refectory became the main hall and the nave of the church became the central block of an impressive gatehouse with oriels over the outer entrance and four octagonal turrets with crossloops in those facing the field.

Wriothesley survived the fall of his master Thomas Cromwell in 1540. He was created Baron Titchfield and Lord Chancellor in 1544 and, as one of the governing council for the young Edward VI, he became Earl of Southampton in 1547. Both Edward VI and Elizabeth I were entertained at Titchfield by his successor Henry, 2nd Earl, and the 4th Earl entertained Charles I there in 1625, and again in 1647, when the king was fugitive from the victorious Parliamentary forces. The house afterwards passed to the Noel family and then to the dukes of Beaufort. It was sold to the Delme family in 1741 and in 1781 most of the building was dismantled. The ruins were handed over to state care in 1923 and are now maintained by English Heritage.

WARBLINGTON CASTLE   SU 729055

Of the house built here by Margaret Pole, Countess of Salisbury between 1514 and 1526, on the site of a moated house for which Edward III granted a crenellation licence to the Monthermer family in the 1340s, only one of the four octagonal corner turrets of the brick gatehouse remains, along with traces of the moat. The gatehouse was of three storeys with typical Tudor four-centred arches. The turret is one stage higher and was probably left standing as a navigational beacon. The countess was eventually executed on a charge of treason by Henry VIII. Her house passed to the Cotton family in 1551 and was probably visited by Elizabeth I in 1586. Described in 1642 as a stronghouse, it was destroyed after being besieged and captured by a Parliamentary force under Sir William Waller during the winter of 1643-4.

WINCHESTER CASTLE   SU 478296   O

Winchester was an important seat of government under the Late Saxon and Norman kings and the castle is assumed to have been founded by William I. However it seems that the palace that he built in 1066-7, which was destroyed be fire in 1141, lay closer to the cathedral. Traces of a strong tower reported to have been found at the south end of Market Street may be associated with this second building. Stigand, the last Saxon Archbishop of Canterbury is said to have been confined in the castle in 1070. The castle was rebuilt in stone by Henry II and his sons Richard and John, who between them are known to have spent at least £1685 upon it, much of the work being done in the 1170s, when the curtain wall and chapel are mentioned. Richard I held court at Winchester in conjunction with his recoronation in 1194 following his release from captivity after being captured during his return from the Holy Land and in 1195-6 there is a mention of repairs to the keep. The castle was captured by Prince Louis of France and the rebel barons in 1216 after a fortnight's siege, but it was recaptured by William Marshall for the young Henry III the following year.

Henry III, who was born in the castle in 1207, frequently held court at Winchester during the Christmas period. Considerable rebuilding was required to repair walls breached during the conflicts of 1216-7 and several new round towers were added and a barbican on the west, whilst the hall was remodelled into its present form. The castle long remained in use as a royal residence, but James I, who had resided at the castle in 1603 when London was affected by the plague, eventually granted it to Sir Benjamin Tichborne. The castle held a Royalist garrison during the Civil War until captured in 1645. By 1651 the buildings and defences had been demolished except for the hall and the site was granted to Sir William Waller. In 1656 he sold the hall for use as the county court for the sum of £100. It remained in use as such until the completion of new courts further east in 1874. Notable trials which took place in the hall included those of Sir Walter Raleigh, condemned as a traitor in 1603, Captain John Burley, sentenced to a traitor's death in 1647 for attempting to rescue Charles I from captivity on the Isle of Wight, and Alice Lisle, who was sentenced by the infamous Judge Jefferys to be burnt to death for harbouring rebels during the Monmouth Rebellion of 1685. The jury were reluctant to convict her and in the end her sentence was commuted to beheading. Charles II eventually recovered the castle site and in 1683 began building a palace in the middle of the site of the castle bailey. It was left incomplete at his death in 1685 and later was adapted as a barracks. These were destroyed by fire in 1894 and the present brick buildings are of c1900.

The round tower base at Winchester

The great hall at Winchester

The walled city of Winchester had its defences mostly following the lines of those of the Roman city of Venta Belgarum. The land rises gently from the River Itchen on the east, where lies the bishop's fortified palace of Wolvesey (see pages 60-61) to the west, and the castle occupied most of the west side south of the still surviving West Gate. This structure is of 13th century origin but its outer face (which was flush with the outer face of the main wall) was remodelled as part of a general repair programme to the walls begun in the 1370s. A new archway was then provided with a pair of keyhole-shaped gunports above, over which are two shields set upon quatrefoils with hood-mounds with head stops, and then at the top there is a row of five machicolations on triple-stepped corbels set between two buttresses. The north, south and east gates were destroyed in 1791. The only other surviving gateway, Kingsgate, is a 14th century structure opening off the cathedral close. In the church of St Swithun above it are modest later medieval windows. Fragments of the walls remain in places, the best section being in College Street, near King's Gate. The Hermit's Tower at the NW corner is modern but on the site of an original tower.

The castle walls enclosed a wedge-shaped area 230m long from north to south by about 55m wide. At the south end there seems to have been a small triangular inner ward (forming the point of the wedge-shape) which is assumed to have been built around what remained of the original motte. It appears that this inner ward had a north-facing gatehouse, two rectangular towers probably of the 1170s at the western corners, and the St Catherine's Tower of c1249-52 at its NE corner, whilst another 13th century circular tower containing a prison in its basement lay between this tower and the SW corner. Charles II's palace lay in the middle of the site and had north and south wings and a long block on the west side against where there had formerly been a gatehouse of the 1240s with a long barbican extending out from it across the 50m width of the outer ditch here. On the east side were two semi-circular towers, the tower behind the king's chapel mentioned in 1241-6 and another tower which is mentioned in the 1250s, although it was probably built somewhat earlier.

The great hall at Winchester

This second tower adjoined the SE corner of what is now the largest and finest castle hall still surviving fully roofed in England, although the exterior has seen considerable rebuilding. Surpassed only by the hall of Westminster Palace, it mostly dates from 1222-36. It measures 33m by 16.5m internally and is of five bays with aisles formed by rows of pointed arches on octofoil-shaped piers of Purbeck marble. Each bay contained on each side a window with two trefoil headed lights with a quatrefoil above. The two east bays contained short windows with doorways below them and the other bays had longer windows with transoms, but in 1845 a new doorway was provided in the middle bay on the north side and the eastern windows were then lengthened. The roundels set between the southern windows originally lay in dormers over the windows until the roof was remodelled in the late 14th century. At the west end of the hall are remains of the dias and a doorway to a staircase to a solar, in a former block which together with the hall, would have once closed off the northern end of the main ward as a small private court. Just 13m beyond the hall north wall lies the base of a 12th century tower keep 16m square. Adjoining its west side was a chapel built in 1220-23. Of the same date is the basement of a 12m diameter tower forming the NE corner of the castle. Steps led down from the keep to a chamber from which passages led off to two sallyports, once facing east into the city and another facing NE towards the ditch of the city wall.

Machicolations on Winchester West Gate

*The West Gate
at Winchester*

Wolvesey Castle

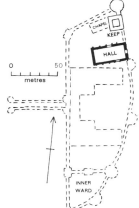

Winchester: hall plan

Hung high up on the west end wall of the hall is the famous round table of King Arthur 5.5m in diameter with places for the king and 24 named knights. The table was regarded as old even in the early 15th century and it was probably installed by Henry III, although it has been repainted several times over the years. Originally it stood on multiple legs. Henry VII's oldest son was born in the castle in 1486 and named Arthur in memory of the legend. The death of this prince at Ludlow in 1502 made the future Henry VIII his father's heir.

Winchester: plan

Wolvesey Castle

WOLVESEY CASTLE   SU 486291   E

Near the River Itchen at the east end of the medieval city of Winchester lie the ruins of the bishop's palace, established here in Saxon times. Not much remains of the block known as the west hall, built c1110 by William Giffard, second of the Norman bishops. Most of the ruins date from the time of Henry de Blois, who was appointed bishop in 1129. The see was the wealthiest in England and de Blois was one of the most noteworthy of its holders. By 1141, when it was unsucessfully besieged by the Empress Matilda, his palace at Wolvesey had been given defences and a second hall, making it one of the finest residences in England at that date. Later bishops only needed to keep it in repair and only minor modifications were made, but in any case later bishops preferred their other residences or accompanied the king's court as holders of major state offices. Some damage may have been done to the palace by Henry II in 1155, when the bishop was out of favour and his castles were confiscated and slighted, but repairs were executed between 1158 and Bishop Henry's death in 1171. The palace was captured by Prince Louis and the rebel barons in 1216 but retaken by William Marshall in 1217. After their marriage in Winchester Cathedral in 1554 Queen Mary and Philip II of Spain held their wedding banquet in the palace at Wolvesey. The palace suffered some damage in the Civil War, and, although a few repairs were made in 1660, it was superseded by a new palace erected over the site of the south end of the western hall block in 1684. See page 59.

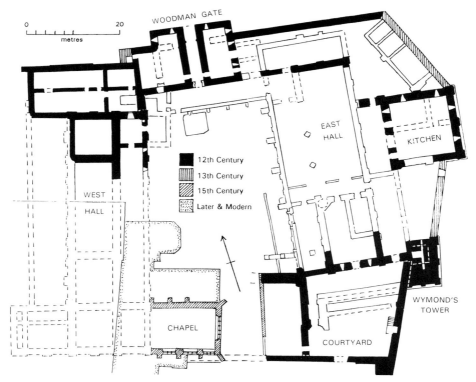

Plan of Wolvesey Castle

The plan of the west hall is known only from excavations during the 1970s. It had a central block about 10m wide and 50m long containing various private rooms for the bishop, set one level above the courtyard but with the space underneath filled with earth. There was a raised garden west of it and a two storey aisle or corridor on the east side. The latrine block at the north end was added later in the 12th century. Projecting west from the south end was a three storey tower containing the bishop's treasury, chapel, and bedchamber. This part was remodelled in the 1370s. A 15th century chapel built by Bishop Beaufort on the site of an original chapel extending eastward on the other side of the building still survives attached to the new palace of 1684. It has a five light east window and three-light south windows.

The east hall containing the bishop's public hall occupied the northern two thirds of a block 43m long by 12m wide and additionally had a 13th century west aisle with a three bay arcade and a lean-to roof. The fourth bay was flanked by a NW porch opening into the aisle, although the public entrance lay at the SE corner. The main hall north end wall has blind arcading. Private rooms lay over the service rooms at the south end. East of here lies Wymond's Tower, a building about 9m square with pilaster buttresses at the corners and middle of the outer sides. It provided latrines discharging outside the outer wall. Pilasters also appear on the hall walls and on those of the keep-like kitchen block, a building 15m square over walls 1.8m thick lying east of the east hall. The kitchen in the southern half of this building extended up to the roof and has evidence of huge fireplaces. From here a curtain wall extended round to the Woodman's Gate on the north side of the palace. Probably built in the 1160s, this structure had a pair of rectangular towers flanking a central passage closed by a drawbridge raised by a counterweight in a stone-lined pit. Despite its ambitious plan this gateway never formed the main entrance and in the 1370s the upper rooms were remodelled to provide accommodation for the bishop's treasurer, the present fireplaces and windows being of that period. The actual main entrance was a more modest gatehouse on the south side. The buildings were surrounded firstly by a moat and then by a low outer wall around an outer court as big as 200m long on the northern side. Separated from the cathedral close by the mill race, this court contained outbuildings such as barns, stables and the bishop's prison.

WOODGARSTON RINGWORK   SU 584551

Behind the farm is a ringwork with traces of a bailey. Probably built by Hugh de Pont c1070-80, this may be the "Castle of the Wood" stormed by King Stephen in 1147.

Wolvesey Castle

GAZETTEER OF CASTLES ON THE ISLE OF WIGHT

CARISBROOKE CASTLE   SZ 488878   E

This castle is recorded in the Domesday Book of 1086 and was then in the king's hands after the forfeiture of Roger, son of William Fitz-Osbern, Earl of Hereford. William is assumed to have built the castle during the short period (1067-1071) that he held the Isle of Wight. Soon after his accession in 1100 Henry I granted the island to Richard de Redvers. In 1136 his son Baldwin fled to the Isle of Wight after surrendering Exeter to King Stephen after a three month siege. His castle at Carisbrook is decribed by a contemporary as being "built of hewn stone", so Baldwin must have rebuilt it since his father's death in 1107. King Stephen besieged the castle, and Baldwin was obliged to submit and go into exile when the water supply failed. He was only restored to his estates in 1153, two years before his death. His elder sons Baldwin II and Richard died without heirs in 1162 and 1184 respectively, after which Carisbrooke went to a younger son, William de Vernon, who built the existing hall. After his great-grandson Baldvin IV died (supposedly of poison) in 1262, the castle passed to the latter's sister Isabel. Recently widowed on the recent death of William de Fortibus, Earl of Albemarle, she was then the richest woman in England outside of the royal family. After her death in 1293 the castle reverted to the Crown and, apart from being held by Piers Gaveston in 1308-9, remained in royal hands.

In 1355 Edward III granted the castle to his daughter Isabel, who married Ingram de Couci. He later sided with the French (who made an unsuccessful attack on the castle in 1377) and was forced to surrender his English estates to Richard II, who in 1385 granted the Isle of Wight to William de Montacute, Earl of Salisbury. This grant was not hereditary and in 1397 Richard II was able to make a fresh grant of the lordship to Edward, Earl of Rutland. The lordship was later held by Humphrey, Duke of Gloucester from 1431 until his attainder for treason in 1446, the Dukes of Somerset until the attainder of Duke Henry in 1461, and Anthony Wydville, Lord Scales, who in turn was removed and attainted when Richard III took the throne in 1483. From the time of Henry VIII onwards the lordship remained with the Crown although the island was effectively ruled by whosoever was appointed as captain of the castle. The title of Governor of the Isle of Wight began to be used with the appointment of Sir George Carey in 1582. He remodelled much of the domestic buildings and added new outer ramparts and bastions for defenced by cannon.

Carisbrooke Castle

Shell keep at Carisbrooke

The old doors in the gateway at Carisbrooke

During the Civil War the Parliamentary faction on the Isle of Wight managed to oust the Royalist Governor, the Earl of Portland. His wife stayed on at the castle with a few friends and servants until she managed to secure good terms for a surrender. In 1647 King Charles was sent to Carisbrooke to be kept in honourable confinement in the castle under the control of Colonel Hammand. Two escape attempts failed, a Captain Burley being excecuted for his part in the first one. A second failed when the king found himself unable to squeeze between the bars of his upper window, having failed to try this before the attempt. A bar was removed for a third attempt but this in turn was foiled as the authorities seem to have got wind of the escape plans. The king was later removed to the Grammar School at Newport, and then later taken off to London for his trial and execution early in 1649.

In 1650 two of Charles' younger children were sent to the castle. Princess Elizabeth died after a few weeks but Prince Henry remained there until sent to Flanders (his sister was Princess of Orange) early in 1653. The castle remained in use as an occasional residence of the governor of the Isle of Wight until the death in 1944 of Princess Beatrice, youngest daughter of Queen Victoria, who had succeeded her husband Prince Henry of Battenberg as governor in 1896. After the war the governor's house was briefly used as a youth hostel before become the Isle of Wight museum, opened in 1951. The castle is now managed by English Heritage.

Domestic buildings at Carisbrooke

The castle has a high mound lying in the north corner of an almost rectangular bailey 120m by 115m, the sides of which bow out slightly, and which is defended by an early 12th century curtain wall 2.2m thick rising up to 5m above an 8m high rampart fronted by a ditch. To the NE is a second slightly smaller bailey with ramparts and later corner bastions. Surrounding all these works are Elizabethan artillery fortifications begun in 1587 in readiness for the Armada but not completed until shortly before the queen died in 1603. Arrow-head shaped bastions or bulwarks with sides up to 70m long flank an outer rampart with an inner ditch in front. An outer ditch then fronts both this and the outer sides of the bulwarks. The east bulwark has recessed flanks containing sallyports and gunports, and the adjacent sides of the north and south bulwark are similarly provided. The bulwark at the NW corner is smaller and perhaps earlier than the others and on the west side there are two lengths of outer curtain with a fifth bulwark between them. This commands the outer gateway over which are initials of Queen Elizanbeth and the date 1598.

The ramparts of the main bailey have at their base outside walling up to 1.5m high of a Roman or Saxon fort. The walling was probably only a front face to an earth rampart. On the NE side are traces of a round turret and of an unturned gateway. Between these two points the 12th century curtain wall has at a later period been extended out and built up above the footings of the fort wall. This section has a narrow postern and ends against the motte in a 14th century turret. Slight traces suggest that the curtain had a square tower in the middle of this side. Other original open-backed towers about 8m wide lie at the east and south corners. The interior of the south tower is still open but otherwise these towers are now embedded within earth-filled stone polygonal bastions of begun in 1587 but not completed until 1601 and 1602, the dates that appear on them. Because these towers were located at points where the curtain wall turned through a corner with several faces the towers would not have flanked the main lengths on intermediate wall, although between them a turret projects about 1m. A 16th century fireplace backs onto its inner side.

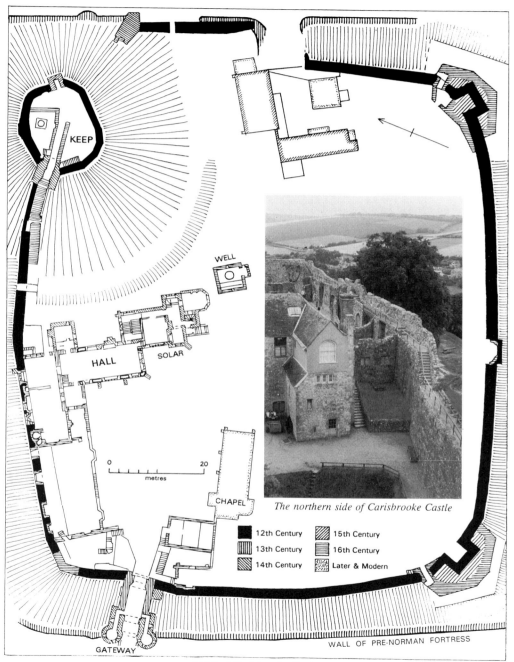

KEEP

WELL

HALL SOLAR

0   20
metres

CHAPEL

The northern side of Carisbrooke Castle

	12th Century		15th Century
	13th Century		16th Century
	14th Century		Later & Modern

WALL OF PRE-NORMAN FORTRESS

GATEWAY

Plans of Carisbrooke Castle

The barbican at Carisbrooke

East of a postern on the north side of the motte ditch a long flight of steps ascends the mound to an oval shell keep with a wall up to 2m thick and 4m high to the wall walk enclosing a court 17.5m by 13.2m. The shell wall appears to be contemporary with the curtain wall, although since the wall facing the bailey is thinner, with straight sides and a plinth, whilst the part facing the outside is curved, with a stepped projection in the middle, there is a possibility that these parts are of different date. The small square NE turret and the two fireplace (one with an oven) set back to back nearby are later medieval and the gatehouse with its portcullis groove and rebate for two sets of doors is 14th century. The part of the interior walled off in the 16th century to contain the 50m deep well was roofed, and another wall parallel to it continues the gatehouse passage into the interior. The shell wall contains an original latrine recess next to the gatehouse.

The curtain wall makes an inturn where it adjoins the gatehouse on the west side of the bailey. The 13th century gatehouse projected mostly within the curtain wall. Of it there there remain only the outer arch, which has a portcullis groove and a pair of 15th century wooden doors. In the 14th century a barbican with an outer gateway with two more portcullises was added in front of this. This part is flanked by two round turrets 4m in diameter containing rooms with crossloops below and key-hole shaped gunloops above. Between the turrets at the top is a row of machicolations. These upper parts are of the 1380s, but they bear on the parapet the arms of Lord Scales added in the 1470s, whilst the lower parts are thought to be of the 1330s. The corner of the curtain wall nearby to the north is a 16th century rebuilding.

The castle buildings mostly lie between the gatehouse and the motte ditch, and the rest of the interior forms gardens, except for a group of much rebuilt late medieval buildings and their yard on the east side. Abutted against the NW section of the curtain is a series of ruined buildings, mostly 16th century, although one of the several windows cut here through the curtain is clearly 13th century, with trefoil headed lights with a transom and seats in the embrasure. West of the chamber here (later converted into a kitchen with ovens in the NW corner) lay lodgings with bow windows facing the court (possibly on the site of the kitchen built in 1287), and east of it lay the buttery and pantry. The latter served a hall 17m long by 6.4m wide in a block extending to the SE. This now has late medieval buttresses and the top storey is a 16th century addition, but a window with twin lancets on the NE side blocked by the late 14th century fireplace breast shows that the hall is essentially a structure of c1200, although the service bay may be a 13th century addition. It has doorways of that date to later wings, one of which contains a staircase and the other a porch.

Projecting NE from the hall east corner is a block of c1270 which originally contained the chapel of St Peter, vaulted in two bays. It now houses a wide staircase. Adjoining this is a three storey late 14th century block containing the great chamber over a kitchen, with two other rooms beyond. A buttress bears the Montague arms. The great chamber has fine original fireplace and a squint looking into the former chapel. At the far end is a staircase projection next to a modern porch. Another room added later beside this projection has a modern bow front. Beyond it lies the well which is housed in a 16th century building containing a donkey-powered wheel for raising water from the great depth. SE of the gatehouse lie the armoury and an office, both 16th century, and the chapel of St Nicholas, a rebuild of c1900-5 on the foundations of a 13th century building.

EAST COWES CASTLE   SZ 511965

Nothing remains of this small artillery fort begun by Henry VIII in 1539. It is said to have been similar to the fort at West Cowes. The house built by John Nash in 1798 and known as East Cowes Castle stood on or near the site and has in turn vanished.

QUARR ABBEY   SZ 566926

The north (or seaward facing) side of the rectangular precinct wall surviving from the former Cistercian Abbey contains a blocked gateway and two gunports of a crude early type. Edward III licensed the wall crenellations in 1365, since the postion of the abbey made it vulnerable to French raids. Little survives of the abbey buildings.

SANDOWN CASTLE   SZ 605846

Henry VIII's records for 1545 include payments of £500 and £600 for work on a fort here. It soon suffered from coastal erosion and a new earth fort was built nearby.

WEST COWES CASTLE   SZ 494966

This fort begun in 1539 by Henry VIII now serves as a sailing club-house, having been much altered in 1856-7 to designs by Anthony Salvin. The semi-circular gun-platform on the seaward side still remauins but the low round tower seems to have been rebuilt. It has an 18th century stair turret and a 19th century NW tower.

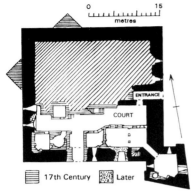

Plan of Yarmouth Castle

Yarmouth Castle

WORSLEY'S TOWER   SZ 333894

A small octagonal tower was built here in the 1520s by Sir James Worsley, Governor of the Isle of Wight, to control the western entrance to the Solent. Its position below a cliff made it vulnerable to overland attack and it was superseded in the 1540s by forts at Yarmouth nearby and Hurst on the opposite shore.

YARMOUTH CASTLE   SZ 354898   E

This artillery fort was begun by Henry VIII in 1545 and completed after the king's death in 1547. It differs from his other forts in being a square of about 30m, washed by the sea on the north and west sides, and having an arrowhead-shaped SE corner bastion flanking the other two sides, which were protected by a wet moat. The north side of the interior was later filled up with earth to make a platform for heavy guns. The south side contains a range of buildings, with a narrow court between the two. The eastern part of the range contained the Master Gunner's House, whilst the western part, built or rebuilt in 1632, contained lodgings for the other gunners, and a new entrance, with a long room above. The original entrance with a double-chamfered four-centred arch surmounted by the royal arms lies in the east wall. Repairs were executed in 1587, 1600-3, and 1609, but further works were said to be needed in the 1620s. Captain Baraby Burley intended to hold the castle for King Charles in 1642 but surrendered on condition he was allowed to remain in residence. The garrison of an officer and 30 men was doubled in 1650, and had been increased to 70 men by 1654. the garrison was disbanded in 1661 but four men still remained when a survey was made in 1669. There was a garrison composed of a captain, master gunner and five men in 1781. The castle was repaired in 1855 and in 1898 was handed over to the coastguard. It is now maintained by English Heritage.

BATH TOWN DEFENCES   ST 748648   F

Upper Borough Walls on the north side and Lower Borough Walls on the south side delineate the size of a small oval walled town within a bend of the Avon. The shape is unusual for defences of assumed Roman origin. The streets of Northgate, Westgate and Southgate are named after vanished gates, and originally the circuit had six gateways. The walls are not mentioned during the attack on Bath in 1088 but they existed by 1138, when the town was garrisoned for King Stephen. A 2m high short section of the wall with the road at wall-walk level survives in Upper Borough Walls.

BRIDGWATER CASTLE   ST 300373   V

Between the Watergate Hotel and the next building to the north of it is a segmental-headed narrow gateway facing West Quay on the west bank of the River Parrett, not far north of the bridge. Beyond is a length of possible curtain walling 5m high. Nothing else remains of the castle, which was captured by the Royalists in June 1643, and destroyed after being captured by Parliamentary troops in 1645. King's Square lies on its site, the earliest buildings there being laid out by the Duke of Chandos in the 1660s. King John issued a licence for the castle to be fortified by William Brewer in 1200 but it was probably founded earlier since it had a motte upon which stood a tower which was repaired in 1242. The castle partly relied on water defences, as did the town, which Leland describes as having four gates. In 1248 Henry III granted the castle to William de Cantilupe, whose wife Eva was a Brewer co-heiress. It later passed to the Mortimers, who rarely used the castle although the hall roof was repaired in 1391, and then via the Duke of York to the Crown in 1461.

BURROW MUMP   ST 359305   F

This former island in marshland is said to have been occupied by Alfred the Great. Foundations of a possible Norman tower were uncovered below remains of a medieval chapel in the 1930s. A castle here is mentioned in the 14th century.

BURY CASTLE   SS 938270

A small motte lies inside a strongly fortified bailey with a counterscarp bank beyond its ditch. The site lies on a ridge between the River Exe and the River Haddeo.

CASTLE CARY   ST 641322   F

This castle is first mentioned in 1138 when King Stephen starved the garrison into submission. It was again besieged on his behalf in 1147 by Henry de Tracy. A siegework being erected was destroyed by a relieving force led by Robert, Earl of Gloucester. The castle may have been founded in the late 11th century by Robert Percival and remained in his family until it passed by marriage to the St Maurs in 1351, by which time the buildings were probably decayed if not actually abandoned. It later passed to Lord Zouche of Harringworth and after his attainder by Richard III went to Lord Willoughby de Broke. By the time the manor was purchased by the first Duke of Somerset in the 16th century a new manor house had been built below the castle. The site lies on the end of a ridge east of the village street and has a ringwork above a pond at the south end and a bailey 90m long by 70m wide on the north with a substantial east rampart and ditch. In the 60m diameter ringwork lie buried the foundations of an ashlar-faced keep 25m by 23m over walls 4.5m thick with a forebuilding in the middle of the north side and an internal crosswall. See pp 4 & 70.

The ringwork at Castle Cary

CASTLE NEROCHE ST 272158 F

On a north-facing spur of a high ridge are extensive earthworks of a presumably once-important castle, but without any recorded history. A farm occupies much of the original main enclosure 90m long by 70m wide, protected on the SE and SW sides by a double rampart and ditch system. To the SE is a larger outer enclosure with a single rampart, now partly occupied by a car park. The high motte north of the farm is thought to have been a later addition. The overgrown summit about 30m across once had a curtain wall. Another enclosure lies beyond to the north.

CREWKERNE: CASTLE HILL ST 421107

12th century pottery has been found on the surface of the Castle Hill.

CULVERHAY CASTLE ST 719631 V

An oval stone-reveted platform 65m by 37m with a counterscarp to its ditch lies on a north-facing spur east of English Combe. It lies on the line of Wansdyke and could be pre-Norman. Footings of a round structure inside it may be a relic of a dovecote.

DONYATT MOAT ST 343145

In 1329 Edward II granted a pardon for the offence of crenellating a building on this moated site without obtaining permission.

Dunster Castle

DUNSTER CASTLE SS 992434 O

William I gave an estate here to William de Mohun and he is assumed to have established the castle which is recorded here in the Domesday Survey of 1086 under the name Torre. An isolated hill, so obvious a site for a fortification that it may have been used as such from a much earlier date, was scarped into a motte with a bailey perched on its eastern slope. William de Mohun II held the castle against King Stephen and successfully withstood a siege by Henry de Tracy in 1139. Nothing remains of the siegework erected by de Tracy. Stephen's rival the Empress Matilda granted de Mohun an earldom (of Somerset) but Stephen never recognised the title and it was not used by further generations of the family. The earliest surviving stone buildings are the remnants of a curtain wall with D-shaped flanking towers probably built by Sir Reynold de Mohun in the 1240s or 50s. Sir John de Mohun, who inherited Dunster in 1330, when aged about ten was the sixth heir in a century and a half to inherit before attaining his majority. He served with Edward III in France and was nominated in 1348 as one of the original 25 knights of the Garter. He made over Dunster to his wife Joan and in 1376, the year after her husband's death, she sold the castle to Lady Elizabeth Luttrell. The contract allowed Joan to remain in residence and in the event she outlived Lady Elizabeth, dying in 1404. The Mohuns were reluctant to hand over the castle and Sir Hugh Luttrell had to take his case to court. He built the outer gatehouse in 1420, after the dispute was settled in his favour.

Outer gatehouse at Dunster

The inner gateway at Dunster

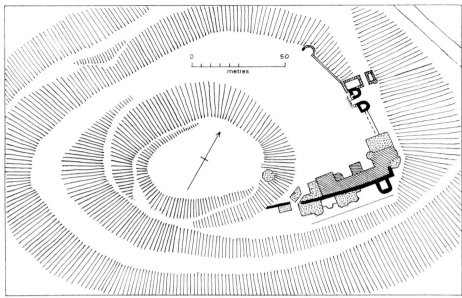

Plan of Dunster Castle

After Sir James Luttrell died of wounds received fighting on the Lancastrian side at Wakefield in 1461, Dunster was confiscated by Edward IV and given to Sir William Herbert, later created Earl of Pembroke. After Richard III's defeat and death at Bosworth in 1485 Sir Hugh Luttrell recovered the castle from Pembroke's successor. Sir Hugh preferred to live at East Quantoxhead and the castle probably lay neglected until the domestic buildings were remodelled by George Luttrell, who died in 1629. The contract between George and the architect William Arnold dates from 1617 but the coat of arms dated 1589 in the hall suggests a possible earlier remodelling.

Thomas Luttrell and his wife held the castle against a Royalist force led by the Marquess of Hertford in 1642. An attack by Welsh Royalists in January 1643 was also beaten off, but after Hertford and Prince Maurice took Taunton in June of that year Thomas Luttrell agreed to surrender Dunster. Prince Charles spent a fortnight at the castle in May 1645. Colonel Wyndham withstood a siege by Colonel Blake from November 1645 until he surrendered on very favourable terms in April 1646. The garrison held out after the walls were breached by mining and in February a relieving force brought in fresh supplies. In 1650, during the time when the pamphleteer William Prynne was kept a prisoner in the castle, Parliament commenced the demolition of the defences, but before this was completed there was a change of heart and a garrison was kept in the fortress until 1651. George Luttrell made his peace with Cromwell and was appointed Sheriff of Somerset in 1652.

The apartments were refurbished in the 1680s for Francis Luttrell and his wife Mary Tregonwell, heiress of Milton Abbas. When Alexander Luttrell died in 1737 he left a young daughter Margaret. She married her cousin Henry Fownes, who took the additional name of Luttrell. A new deer park was laid out and a new breakfast and withdrawing room were created c1770. The buildings owe much of their present appearance to a rebuilding begun in 1867 by Anthony Salvin for George Fownes Luttrell. His great-grandson Walter gave the castle to the National Trust in 1976.

The domestic buildings at Dunster

In early medieval times the sea came right up to the base of the hill on which the castle stands. Nothing remains of the defences of an oval court about 60m long by 40m wide which stood on the highest part of the hill, the only structure there now being an octagonal summer house of 1727. The ground level of the bailey 90m long by 40m wide was raised in 1764 to create the Green Court. The curtain wall rose from a ditch, now filled in. It has vanished at the north end but parts remain in the house and a 5m high section stands west of it at the foot of the mound. One D-shaped tower remains in ruins beyond the gateway, although all the thin walling above courtyard level seems to be later rebuilding. The gateway is flanked by two D-shaped towers about 6m in diameter. The guard room in the lowest storey of the northern tower has three cross-shaped arrow-loops facing the field. The outer gatehouse of the 1420s projects out in front of this tower, and is partly built over the top of it. Originally a curtain wall must have closed off a small court or barbican between the two gateways. The outer gateway has a vaulted passage flanked by rooms and two upper storeys with two-light windows. A polygonal turret on the SE corner leads to the upper rooms but the topmost storey, which is level with the main court, has a doorway direct from the court in its west end wall. The octagonal turrets at this end date from 1764 when the upper room was remodelled to provide the Tenants' Hall, in which estate business could be conducted.

The main house lying on the south side of the bailey contains work of several periods. The Inner Hall lies on the site of the original medieval great hall and contains a fine ceiling and an overmantel dated 1589. The Outer Hall into which the porch opens was created by Salvin in 1870-1. Adjoining the hall NE corner is a tower-like embattled wing added by Salvin as an extension of an earlier structure in which lies the Dining Room (originally the Great Parlour), with its splendid plaster ceiling of 1681. This wing has a spiral stair in a polygonal turret on one side. A wider main stair of the 1680s is provided in a medieval U-shaped tower projecting from the middle of the inner hall. Further west is a second tower added by Salvin with a diagonally placed turret on the SE corner. It replaced an 18th century chapel. The room said to have been used by Prince Charles lies in a NW wing which contained the service rooms in the medieval layout, the Billiard Room below having once been the kitchen.

FARLEIGH HUNGERFORD CASTLE   ST 801576   E

The manor was once known as Farleigh Montfort after that family, which had a house on this site. It was sold to the de Burghersh family and then passed to an heiress, Elizabeth le Despencer who in 1370 sold the manor to Sir Thomas de Hungerford. In 1383 Sir Thomas obtained a pardon from Richard II for fortifying the site without royal permission. His son Sir Walter was summoned to the parliament of 1426 as Baron Hungerford. He added the outer court around the former parish church, which thus became the castle chapel, and a new parish church was built elsewhere. The 3rd Baron Hungerford, took the name Lord Moleyns on account of his wife's inheritance. He was forfeited by Edward IV in 1461, and was captured and executed after the Lancastrian defeat at Hexham, while his elder son Thomas was attained and executed in 1469. A younger son, Walter, finally recovered the castle in 1486, after it had been held for twenty years by Richard, Duke of Gloucester, who on becoming king in 1483, granted Farleigh to John Howard, Duke of Norfolk.

In 1523 Agnes, widow of Walter's son Edward, was hanged for her part in the murder of her first husband John Cotell at Farleigh Castle, the body of the strangled man being burnt on the kitchen fire. The third wife of Sir Edward's son Walter complained of being imprisoned and starved in one of the towers, traditionally the Lady Tower at the SW corner on the inner ward. Walter was attainted and executed in 1540, and the next owner, Thomas Seymour, was in turn was attainted and executed in 1549. Queen Mary sold the castle back to Walter's son, another Walter, in 1554. During the Civil War the castle was owned by Sir Edward Hungerford, a Parliamentarian, who recovered it in September 1645 from a Royalist garrison commanded by his own half-brother John. On Edward's death in 1648 the castle passed to another Royalist half-brother, Anthony Hungerford. His son Edward is said to have entertained Charles II at the castle c1675. Arms and armour were taken from the castle during a raid upon it by Government troops after the discovery of the Rye House Plot. The castle fell into ruin after being sold in 1686 by the spendthrift Edward. An engraving of 1774 shows the castle almost in its present condition, except that the chapel was then derelict. It was sold to the Houltons of Trowbridge in 1730. It has been in State guardianship as an ancient monument since 1915.

Inner ward at Farleigh Hungerford

Outer curtain wall at Farleigh Hungerford

The castle lies on a low promontory with a stream below the north side. The water of a moat around the south and west sides was held in by a dam on the west. Walls up to 1.4m thick, now reduced to foundations, enclosed a court 55m by 48m. Integral with the curtains were blocks of lodgings against the east, west and south sides. A 16th century bakehouse lay against the west part of the north wall but the rest of this wall was fronted by a private garden. Very little remains of a central east-west range containing an upper floor hall with a solar on the east and a kitchen and other service rooms on the west. Near the latter was a well. In the middle of the south side is the base of a gatehouse with a passageway just 2m wide flanked by U-shaped towers 6m wide. In front of it was a 15th century polygonal barbican. East of here the moat has been filled in. The court between the gatehouse and the hall retains its cobbled surface. Each corners of the inner ward had a circular tower, those on the south being 8m in diameter over walls 1.4m thick and still partly standing five storeys high. Of the larger and more massive northern towers only the bases remain far below courtyard level. The NW tower hardly projected beyond the outer walls

The wall of the D-shaped outer court still stands complete except for a short section on the west, together with the SW tower, which are reduced to footings, while just the floor remains of a stable against the south wall. Only fragments remain of the west gate, but the square east gate is nearly complete, although it has modern battlements instead of the four gables it had in the 17th century. There is a square-headed recess for the raised drawbridge with chain holes, between which the sickle badge of the Hungerfords, whose arms appear above with the initials of Sir Edward (c1520). The foundations outside the gateway are of early 17th century buildings. There is a round bastion 7m in diameter on the south side of the court.

On the east side is St Leonard's chapel, a diagonally buttressed rectangle of the mid 14th century which was originally the parish church. The chantry chapel of St Anne on the north side was added by Sir Thomas Hungerford in the 1380s to be his burial place. The east window is also late 14th century, the blocked side windows are 15th century, and the west porch is 16th century. Inside are a 12th century font, wall paintings of the 1440s, and effigies of Sir Thomas Hungerford and his wife Joan and several of their descendants, those of Sir Edmund, d1648, and his wife Margaret Holliday being particularly splendid. The priest's house projecting beyond the curtain wall east of the chapel is 15th century with a 17th century northern extension.

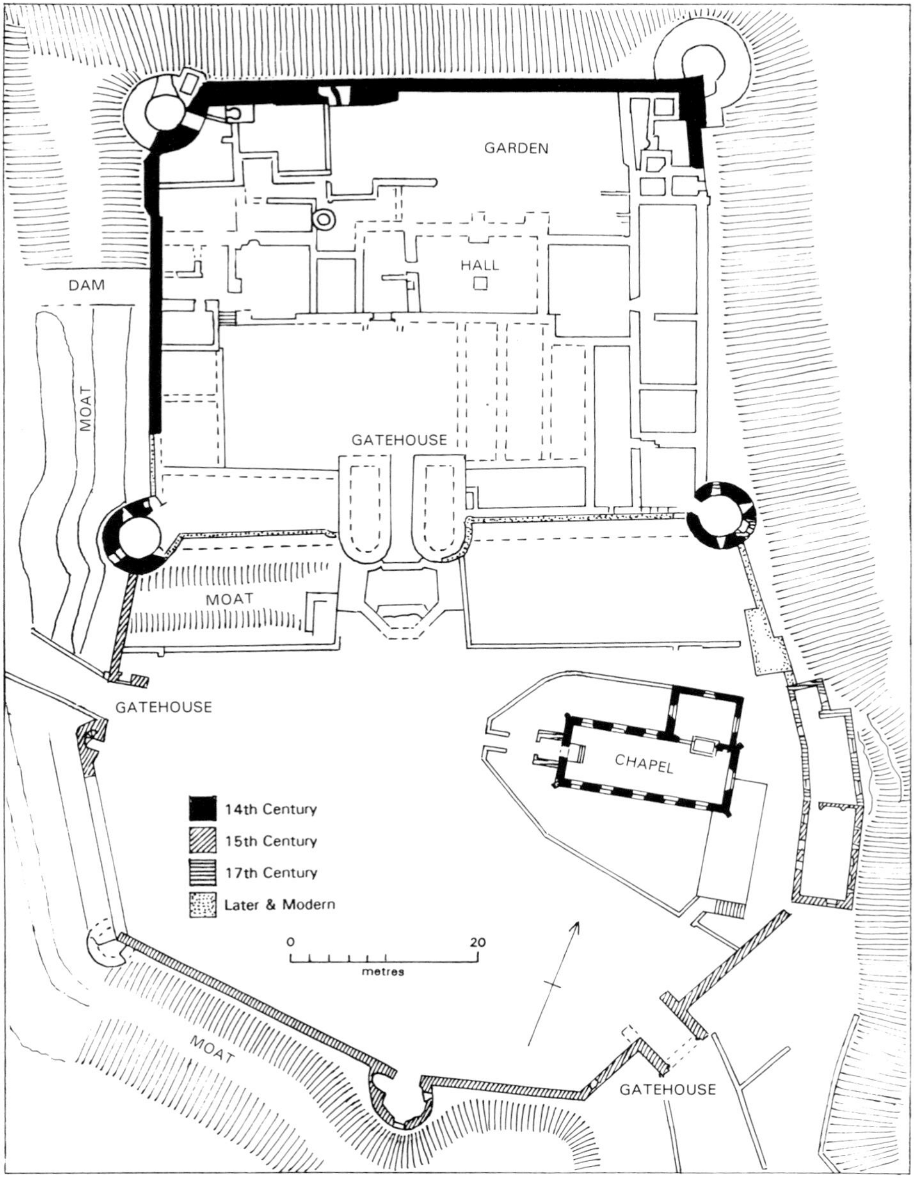

GARDEN

DAM

MOAT

HALL

GATEHOUSE

MOAT

GATEHOUSE

CHAPEL

14th Century
15th Century
17th Century
Later & Modern

0   20
metres

MOAT

GATEHOUSE

Plan of Farleigh Hungerford Castle

FENNY CASTLE   ST 508436

An island in marshland 2km SW of Wookey has been scarped into a small inner
platform and a larger outer platform SE of it. Traces of masonry defences have been
revealed and the site is referred to as a ruin in 1478.

Outer gatehouse at Farleigh Hungerford

GLASTONBURY CASTLE   ST 490386

SW Tower at Farleigh Hungerford

Excavation of the low platform almost surrounded by streams west of the town failed to find medieval remains, so the palace built at Glastonbury by Henry de Blois, Bishop of Winchester, some time between 1127 and 1154 may have been elsewhere.

HALES CASTLE   ST 7977443

This ringwork lies on the NW side of Rodenbury Hill close to the Wiltshire border, 4km SE of Frome.

HARPTREE CASTLE   ST 561557   F

Strongly situated on a wooded promontory between two valleys are two enclosures, the northern or innermost of which seems to have had a curtain wall around a roughly triangular court about 45m across. Part of the base of a circular or D-shaped tower about 10m in diameter remains above a steep drop near the north end of the site. Thomas de Gournay, who died in 1343, was licensed to crenellate by Edward III to crenellate his castle of East Harptree. The castle was captured by King Stephen in 1138, after a siege-castle was built against it, but was retaken by Robert of Gloucester's forces in 1140. There is a further mention of the castle in 1296.

ILCHESTER TOWN DEFENCES

The Roman defences of Ilchester seem to have still been serviceable during the medieval period since Robert de Mowbray was unable to capture the place in 1088 and the walls are mentioned in 1200. No remains now stand above the ground.

LANGPORT TOWN DEFENCES   ST 424267

Langport is thought to have been surrounded by a water filled ditch and rampart in the Saxon period, although the 270m long section of rampart around the north and east sides of the town may be no older than the Civil War period, when Langport was captured by Parliament in 1645. East of the church is the guild chapel known as the Hanging Chapel since executions here in 1685, below which is a town gateway with a pointed tunnel-vault, although it has neither a door rebate or portcullis groove.

LOCKING CASTLE   ST 363609

South of Locking Head Farm are slight traces of a worn-down motte and bailey castle. Excavation of the mound revealed a drystone cellar 2.7m square containing a sword, an oxbone and a pottery fragment.

MONTACUTE CASTLE   ST 493170   F

St Michael's Hill, west of the church, was scarped into a central motte with a summit 50m by 35m towering over a concentric platform 30m wide at a lower level, which was probably divided into several baileys. On the north and west the motte has a ditch with a counterscarp bank. The platform is defended by steep natural slopes except on the east where a ditch divided it from an outer bailey. A Norman garrison withstood an attack by Saxons in 1069. A castle here is mentioned in Domesday Book in 1086, but by 1104 the site had been given to the Cluniac Priory south of the village.

tower window, Newton

Newton St Loe, gateway plan

Newton St Loe: gatehouse

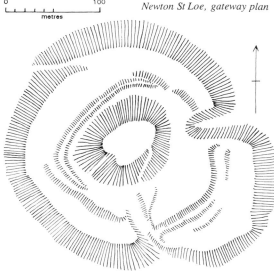

0   100
metres

Plan of Montacute Castle

Remains of keep at Nether Stowey

NETHER STOWEY CASTLE   ST 187396   F

Foundations of a tower keep lie in the centre of the 45m diameter summit of a ditched motte 5m high with two baileys lying to the NE and SE. A church of St Michael once lay below the east end of the SE bailey. The keep measured 16.3m square over walls 2.2m thick with pilaster buttresses in the middle of each side and clasping the corners. Crosswalls divided the basement into two chambers of almost equal size on the east and two more chambers on the west, the smallest room in the NW corner perhaps being a prison. A forebuilding 7m wide projected 6m beyond the south end of the east wall. This tower keep was probably built by Walter de Chandos, lord of Nether Stowey c1120-56. It, or a wooden predecessor, may have been the tower occupied by William Fitz Odo which was captured by Henry de Tracy in 1139 after lighted torches were thrown through the loopholes. See pages 4 & 6.

NEWTON ST LOE CASTLE   ST 694640

In the grounds of Joseph Newton's mansion of Newton Park, built in the 1760s, and now a college, are remains of the castle of the St Loe family. On the west side is a late 15th century gatehouse with a fan-vaulted passage with a portcullis groove in the outer arch. In the arch south jamb is a circular gunport from a guardroom reached from the passage. The parapet is boldly corbelled out, but without machicolations. Added later, and partly blocking two small windows on the upper storey, are buttresses corbelled out at the summit as turrets. No curtain walls survive but a court about 30m by 40m is defined by the land sloping away on the east and north sides and by an embattled tower about 11m by 7.5m at the SE corner. A spiral stair in the middle of the west side has tiny two-light windows set in a re-entrant angle, and leads to three upper storeys each with four-light mullion and transom windows facing east and south with all the lights arched. There is another projection facing north, towards where footings of a probable hall block remain.

The gatehouse at Newton St Loe

The gatehouse at Newton St Loe

NUNNEY CASTLE   ST 737458   F

Sir John de la Mare obtained a licence from Edward III to "fortify and crenellate his manse at Nonny" in 1373 and the building was probably completed before his death ten years later. The style of the building is French and Sir John is assumed to have made his fortune during service in France, although there is no record of this. In c1420 the castle was inherited by Sir John Poulet, son of the grand-daughter of Sir John de la Mare. William Poulet, who died in 1572, rose to become Earl of Wiltshire and Marquis of Winchester. His main seat was Basing House and Nunney was probably neglected until in 1577 it was sold to Richard Prater. He is assumed to have changed the internal arrangements of the tower at Nunney and inserted two-light windows into the lower two levels, which had hitherto only been dimly lighted by narrow loops. The Praters got into a feud with the Mawdleys, who also held land in the parish, and in 1586 they were accused by the Mawdleys in the Court of Star Chamber of assault. After their victory at Sherborne in September 1645 a Parliamentary force attacked Nunney and made a breach in the north wall after a two day bombardment with two cannon. Colonel Richard Prater and his garrison of eight Irishmen under Captain Turbeville then surrendered. There is no evidence that the castle was slighted although it is likely that it was subsequently dismantled by removing the floors, roofs and parapets. Most of the weakened north wall finally collapsed on Christmas Day 1910. The Praters sold the estate to the Whitchurch family c1700. The ruin has been in State guardianship since 1926.

Nunney Castle

Nunney Castle

Nunney: entrance doorway

Plans of Nunney Castle

SE tower at Newton St Loe

The castle is a tower house 23.6m long by 12.2m wide with drum towers 9m in diameter on each corner, these being closely set at the east and west ends. The walls are 2.2m thick, except for the north wall, which contains the entrance at ground level and the stairs, and was slightly thicker. There is now a berm 6m wide between the walls of the main block and the 8m wide wet moat but until the late 16th century the water came right up to the walls. A timber bridge led over to a pier which is now embedded in the berm and then there was a drawbridge which closed up against the doorway. It was above this point that the breach was made in 1645. Beyond the moat on this side there was a court with a wall 3.6m high containing outbuildings.

Nunney Castle

The main block contained a kitchen at ground level with a fireplace in the south wall and a well in a north embrasure. The loop beside the fireplace was widened into a window in the late 16th century. The next storey was reached by a straight stair up from the west jamb of the entrance passage and formed a dark servants hall. Fine two-light windows with pointed heads distinguished the lord's hall on the third storey. Originally there were two of these windows on each side and a large fireplace (now blocked, between those on the south. There is a second fireplace (a later replacement of a medieval one) further east in this wall. The spiral stair serving the upper rooms beside the NE tower was quite narrow and in the 16th century the rooms in this tower were done away with and replaced by a much wider staircase with wooden treads. Originally the third storey room in this tower was an ante-chamber to the hall with a fireplace, whilst the rooms above and below were bedrooms with latrines. The fourth storey of the main block was probably divided into two rooms, the western (or most private) of which had a passage from its west facing window embrasure into a chapel in the SW tower. The chapel has windows facing east and west and a canopied piscina. The two light windows of the top storey are tucked underneath the corbels for a former machicolated parapet carried round the entire building. Within this parapet the towers contained thinly walled fifth storey rooms.

PENSELWOOD CASTLES   ST 753311 & 746323

Balland's Castle, a small motte with a summit about 10m across lies on a east-facing slope 0.5km SW of Penselwood Church. An oval bailey platform 45m long from north to south by 25m wide lies isolated from it to the south. This bailey has a counterscarp to its ditch. Another motte, also with a bailey, lies on a more elevated site in a clearing in Cockroad Wood, 1.2km NW of Penselwood Church. A third site lies just 1km to the NE at Pen Pits in Stourton parish, Wiltshire (see page 100).

STOGURSEY CASTLE ST 203426 V

This castle of the de Courcy (Stogursey is a corruption of Stoke Courcy) family is first mentioned in the 1090s. It was held for King John in 1215 but in the following year the king ordered the Prior of Stogursey Priory to dismantle the castle. However the castle was tenable in 1224, when it was besieged by the Sheriff of Somerset during Faulkes de Breaute's rebellion against Henry III. The castle is said to have been captured in 1455 by Lord Bonville during his conflict with the Courtenay Earl of Devon. It has a wet-moated ringwork 3m high with a thin ruined curtain wall still partly 4m high around a polygonal court about 35m across. There is a D-shaped tower on the west side and on the east are two more towers in a very cut-down state flanking the gateway,. One of these towers still has cross-shaped arrow-loops and is likely to be mid 13th century work but the curtain wall may be 12th century. Rooms in this tower and over the passageway were later remodelled to form a cottage and in recent years this has been renovated by the Landmark Trust to form a holiday home. Beyond the moat there is a bailey platform 30m wide curving round the east and south sides, and these is a larger outer bailey further to the east.

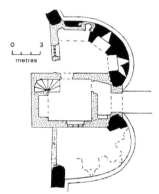

Stogursey: gatehouse plan

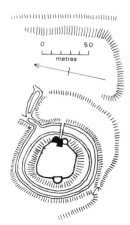

Plan of Stogursey Castle

STOKE-UNDER-HAM CASTLE ST 476177

A licence to crenellate a house here was issued by Edward III in 1334 but it is uncertain whether anything was built as a result of it.

STOWEY SUTTON ST 597593

A large enclosure lies on a ridge SW of the church.

Stogursey Castle

TAUNTON CASTLE   ST 226247   O

Henry de Blois, Bishop of Winchester from 1129 to 1171, and brother of King Stephen, is thought to have begun the rectangular keep in 1138. The hall and solar blocks may be of his time, or could possibly have been built by his predecessor William Giffard as an unfortified residence alongside the Augustinian priory which stood here until it was transferred out of the town in 1158. After King Stephen died in 1154 Bishop Henry fled to France and all his castles were dismantled by Henry II. It was, however, soon rebuilt. The curtain wall around the inner ward seems to have been built in King John's reign by Bishop Peter des Roches. He also laid out the outer bailey to the south. Bishop William Raleigh remodelled the domestic buildings in the 1240s and perhaps walled in stone the outer ward. In 1280 Amory, son of Simon de Montford, Earl of Leicester, who had been defeated and killed at Evesham in 1265, was brought a prisoner to the keep at Taunton from Sherborne Castle. The castle is very low lying on the south bank of the River Tone and in 1326 a large labour force was required to sort out problems caused by flooding. In 1339 the constable, Peter de Grymstede, was dragged out of the castle by a mob. He took refuge in St Mary's church until rescued by the Sheriff of Somerset. Geoffrey Chaucer's son Thomas was appointed constable of the castle in 1408.

In 1451 Thomas de Courtenay, Earl of Devon was besieged in the castle by Lord Bonville until Richard, Duke of York brought a force to its relief. In 1551 the then bishop made over the castle to Edward VI in an exchange of lands. The castle was leased for a few years by Elizabeth I to Sir Francis Knollys but in 1575 it was restored to Bishop Horne. His arms and the date 1577 formerly appeared on the building. Nearly £400 was spent by the Crown on repairs to the castle in 1578. The castle was described in 1635 as "now much ruinated, especially the great tower". Parliament spent £300 on repairing the castle in 1642, fortifying both it and the town. They were occupied by the Royalists in the summer of 1643 but in June 1644 were recovered for Parliament by Colonel Robert Blake after a siege lasting a week. A Royalist force under Sir Edmund Wyndham attacked Taunton in August, breaking into the town, although the castle held out until a relief force arrived from Chichester. In the spring of 1645 Lord Goring attacked Taunton until driven off by a relief force in May. He made another attempt to capture Taunton in June. The north side of the castle was badly damaged by cannonfire during these attacks. The castle was abandoned by Parliament in 1651 but some repairs seem to have been executed in 1651. The restored Charles II regarded Taunton as a place whose loyalty was suspect and he ordered the castle keep destroyed in 1662.

Base of keep at Taunton

East gateway at Taunton

Taunton Castle

After the Duke of Monmouth's defeat at Sedgemoor in 1685 large numbers of the captured rebels were held in the castle. The notorious Judge Jeffreys tried over 500 rebels in just three days in sessions held in the great hall. Several were hanged, drawn and quartered at Taunton and many others were executed in other towns and villages in Somerset. The Beresfords occupied the castle as bailiffs and keepers until they sold their interest to the Lucas family in 1735. The Assizes and Quarter Sessions were held in the castle hall until the Shire Hall was completed in 1857. The castle was purchased in 1874 by the Somerset Archaeological and Natural History Society and still contains their extensive collections.

Only the base (excavated in the 1920s) remains of the keep which measured 24m by 19m, large enough to contain a hall and chamber side by side over basements. On the west side is a plinth with numerous chamfered steps. The keep lay within the eastern part of a wedge shaped inner ward 80m long by up to 50m wide. Little remains of the eastern part (which is not open to the public) but the western part remains, although much altered. On the NW side is the hall, with typical Norman pilaster buttresses towards the river and a rebuilt stair turret at the NW corner. The 9m wide Norman hall lay over two vaulted cellars but was brought down to ground level in a mid 13th century remodelling. It was lengthened and provided with large mullion-and-transom windows facing north in the late 17th century. In 1786 Sir Benjamin Hammet provided the hall with oval windows lighting galleries and divided it into two rooms, the Nisi Prius Count at the west end and the Crown Court at the east end, whilst a Jury Room (demolished in 1931) was added facing the courtyard.

More typically Norman pilaster buttresses clasp the corners of the rectangular west tower which contained the bishop's solar, the undercroft of which was provided with a vault in the 13th century. The pointed-headed windows date from a remodelling of the whole castle in 1786 when the moat was also filled in. The south front is early 13th century and originally had a round tower at each end. Very little remains of the eastern one, whilst the west tower has two tiers of windows of 1786. The gateway in the middle has a portcullis groove (with a short modern false portcullis) and bears the arms of Bishop Thomas Langton, with the date 1495, and is likely to be of that period, together with a range east of it, although towards the court this range has cross-windows of c1700 and a doorway with a shell-hood. The stair turret on the gatehouse NE corner was rebuilt in 1875. The range west of the gateway originally contained a chapel on the upper storey but was converted to judges' lodgings in 1786. It retains one original lancet on the lower level.

Wells Bishop's Palace

Beyond the 15m wide moat on the south side, now filled in, an outer ward 120m wide extended 90m to the south. Nothing remains of the curtain wall or west gate but the 13th century East Gate still remains adjoining the Castle Hotel, although its upper windows are early 19th century. It has a long passageway with a portcullis groove in the double-chamfered outer arch. The outer ward had probably been abandoned to the town by 1521-1 when Bishop Richard Fox built a schoolhouse on the south side of it. It remained a school until 1887 when it became the offices of Taunton Borough Council.

WELLS: BISHOP'S PALACE   ST 362637   O

The Bishop's Palace lies immediately south of the cathedral and is reached from the Market Place through a gateway built in the early 15th century by Bishop Beckynton. It is more of a castle than most other palaces adjoining cathedrals, having a 5m high curtain wall and a wet moat 10m wide surrounding an irregular pentagonal court about 150m by 120m. There are small round towers at the corners and in the middle of the 135m long SE side. Near the middle of the 60m long NW side is a three storey gatehouse with two polygonal-fronted towers, the eastern of which has a late 16th century oriel at second storey level. There are lions heads on the vaulting of the passageway. Edward III licensed Bishop Ralph of Shrewsbury to erect these defences in 1341. Lying almost in the middle is the ruined hall built by Bishop Robert Burnell in the 1280s, a huge structure 35m long by 18m wide. It had angle turrets and that at the east corner now stands isolated since the adjoining walls are missing. The hall had windows of two lights with transoms and Y-tracery with a sexfoiled circle above at the top. The kitchen lay at the SW end and had a fine chamber above it. Off the NE end was access to the chapel of the same period, a superb room vaulted in three bays with a west window of five stepped lancets and a six-light east window.

Wells Bishop's Palace

Adjoining the chapel NE corner is the original hall block built in the 1230s by Bishop Jocelyn but much rebuilt in 1846 by Benjamin Ferrey for Bishop Bagot, when the central porch and dormer windows were added. This block has a hall and solar over vaulted undercrofts which include a gallery on the west side with a later fireplace. The upper windows have quatrefoils over pairs of trefoiled lights. The main staircase is 17th century but a medieval spiral stair remains in the SW corner. To the north is a kitchen and other service rooms built by Bishop Beckynton, the doorway towards the court having fleurons. Two oriel windows overlooking the moat on the north side can be dated to c1525-35 since they have the arms of Bishop Clark.

WIMBLE TOOT ST 561280

This small mound lies near a stream on flat ground 0.6km SSW of Babcary village.

WORLE: CASTLE BATCH ST 362637 V

This small ringwork on open ground surrounded by the outer suburbs of Weston-super-Mare has a ditch which is partly water-filled.

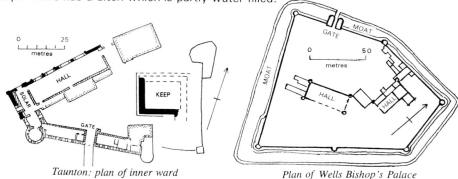

Taunton: plan of inner ward   *Plan of Wells Bishop's Palace*

GAZETTEER OF CASTLES IN WILTSHIRE

ASHTON KEYNES CASTLE   SU 049944

There is a moated site beyond a house south of the church but the castle earthworks, known as Hall's Close, lie 0.5km to the east. A bailey defined by low ramparts lies west of a pentagonal ringwork about 50m across. There is much surface water in the district and this site was clearly once defended by water-filled moats. In 1959 a trial trench found evidence of a wall on the ringwork with pottery from the early 12th century to the 13th century, when the Keynes family occupied this site. It is likely that this was the castle of South Cerney captured by King Stephen in 1139.

BINCKNOLL CASTLE   SU 107793   F

Strongly situated on a north-facing promontory on the downs 7km SW of Swindon is a motte rising 3m to a summit 25m by 20m which is eroded on the SE side. A ditch survives on the west. The triangular bailey extending 100m towards the only approach from the south may be an adaptation of an Iron Age fort. It has a rampart and ditch extending for 100m on the south side to isolate the site. This castle is thought to have been built in the late 11th century by Gilbert of Breteuil.

BISHOPSTROW MOTTE   ST 901440

East of the farm are slight traces of a small mound with outworks to the east and a larger outer enclosure around the whole. A trial excavation in 1981 found two shards of probable 12th century pottery plus much evidence of Iron-Age occupation here.

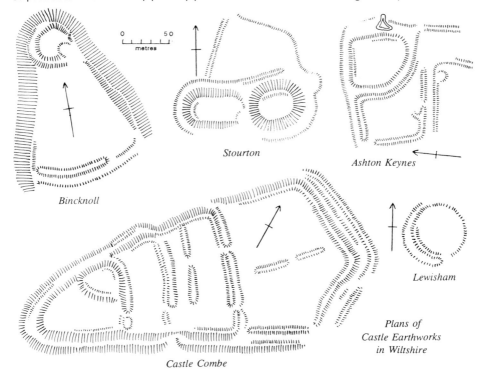

0   50
metres

Stourton

Ashton Keynes

Bincknoll

Lewisham

Castle Combe

Plans of
Castle Earthworks
in Wiltshire

CASTLE COMBE   ST 837777

The site has a total length of 400m from SW to NE and lies 0.4km north of the village and is protected on the west and south by the steep-sided valley of the By Brook. The 90m long inner bailey is triangular with rounded corners with a ringwork 30m across in its northern part. The ringwork is reported to have had a tower measuring about 10m by 9m over walls 3m thick on the SE side. An outer bailey lies to the NE, divided from the inner bailey by a series of banks which appear to be mostly constructed of drystone and are perhaps of Iron Age origin. Castle Combe was a barony from an early date and was probably built by the de Dunstanvilles during Henry I's reign, but the only mention of a castle here is in 1478, when it was said to be derelict.

CASTLE EATON   SU 161965

Leland mentions a castle here beside the Thames, construction of which was licensed by Edward II in 1311. Slight earthworks remain on the Wiltshire bank of the river. Here may have been the site of the castle built in 1144 by William of Dover which was described as having water and marsh on every side.

CHIPPENHAM CASTLE   ST 922732

A large mound is said to have stood west of the market place until the early 19th century. It seems to have adjoined the site of a palace of the Saxon kings.

CRICKLADE TOWN DEFENCES   SU 100935   V

The town lies just west of where the Roman Road from Silchester to Cirencester crossed the River Thames. In the late 9th century King Alfred surrounded the town with a rampart faced with timber and surmounted by timber palisading. The facing of the rampart was later replaced in stone, probably in the early 11th century. Considerable lengths of the 4m high rampart still remain. Nothing survives of a castle built by one of the Empress Matilda's supporters in 1144.

DEVIZES CASTLE   SU 002613

Devizes formed part of the estates of the bishopric of Salisbury and the castle is assumed to have been built by Osmund, nephew of William I, who was made bishop in 1078. The first mention of it is in 1106, when Henry I sent his elder brother Robert to be confined in it for most of the next twenty years. In 1113 the wooden buildings were destroyed by fire and Bishop Roger gradually rebuilt it in stone. In 1139 he was captured by King Stephen and obliged to surrender the castle, then one of the largest and strongest in the realm, and commanded by Roger's nephew Nigel, Bishop of Ely. In 1140 the castle was taken in a surprise attack by Robert Fitz Hubert, whose men scaled the walls with leather ladders. Some of the defenders held out against him in a high tower for another four days. Fitz Hubert had taken the castle for Matilda but he became a freebooter, owing allegiance to neither Matilda nor Stephen, until he was hanged by the Earl of Gloucester after capture by John the Marshall. Stephen made an unsuccessful attack on the castle in 1149, which was then a personal possession of the Empress Matilda. It later passed to her son Henry II, the Bishop of Salisbury being compensated by the king in 1157.

King John spent over £100 on the buildings and ditches during his reign. Another £383 is said to have been spent on the defences in 1237-40 when the castle was commanded by John de Plessis. In 1249 Henry III authorised expenditure of up to £600, and a fireplace was provided in the queen's chamber in 1256.

About £260 was spent on repairs at Devizes in 1328, when there is mention of the king's chamber, a great chamber over a cellar, a wardrobe for royal clothes, a nursery, the queen's larder, the great saucery, and a "cuphous". In 1377-81 there is mention of a kitchen, the tailor's chamber, the squires' chamber, a bakehouse with two ovens, a pantry, a stable for forty horses and an aviary. There were two chapels, that in the inner ward having glazed windows. In this period the south and east parts of the curtain wall were repaired.

In 1411-14 the buildings were repaired to provide a residence for Joan of Navarre, Henry IV's consort. A great tower in the outer ward is then mentioned. The same tower seems to have gained a new door in 1380. The pattern of giving the castle to queen consorts was broken by the tenure of Humphrey, Duke of Gloucester in the period before the marriage of Henry VI and a grant to the Bishop of Salisbury in 1461. By then the curtain walls were "broken", the kitchen was roofless and the bridge over the outer ditch had collapsed, but the bishop was nevertheless in residence in September of that year so the main chambers must have been habitable.

Leland describes the castle as ruinous and mentions that there were once six or seven portcullises. Not long before his visit in c1540 the steward, Sir Edward Baynton, had dismantled part of the inner gatehouse and chapel to provide materials for building work at Bromham House. The castle was said to be "utterly ruinated and decayed" in 1596 but courts continued to be held in one of the chambers until c1615, and in 1619 it was recorded that the bishop still occasionally stayed in the castle. The decayed defences were strengthened by the Royalists in the 1642-4. In September 1645 the castle was besieged and captured by Cromwell, who set up ten cannon in the Market Place to bombard it. Demolition was ordered in 1646 although the work was only completed two years later. The inner gatehouse may have survived until c1700 but all the stone had been used for new construction work in the town by the early 18th century. The castellated mansion built c1840 by the Leach family, and extended in the 1860s and 70s, incorporates part of a brick 17th century tower windmill on the north side.

Most of the west end of a wedge-shaped bailey 220m by 180m was filled with a large ringwork 90m across on top and its. The ground slopes away on all sides except to the east, where the bailey was widest. Here lay the town, which had its own bank and ditch around a kidney-shaped area 400m long from north to south by 200m wide, which was originally an outer ward of the castle. At the south end of this town ward lies the Norman church of St John. About 150m beyond lay an outer bank around both town and castle and a second Norman church, St Mary's lies on the NE side. Upon the ringwork lay a walled polygonal court with solid corner turrets. This surrounded an aisled hall 20m long with circular columns 1m in diameter, footings of it being excavated in 1858-9. The hall seems to have been built in the 1120s or 30s, although it is first mentioned in 1236. There were service rooms at the west end, porches on either side and a tower at the SE corner. East of the hall stood the keep, A few foundations remain in a sunken garden west of the existing building.

DOWNTON CASTLE   SU 181214   F

In a public park on the east bank of the River Avon are confused earthworks of what appear to have been a large ringwork with two semi-circular baileys defending the east side. It was built in 1138 by Henry de Blois, Bishop of Winchester and is thought to have stood close to his unfortified stone-built palace here. The castle was captured in 1148 by followers of the Empress Matilda, but it was soon retaken by the bishop's nephew Hugh de Puiset. Along with the bishop's other fortresses it is assumed to have been demolished by Henry II soon after his accession in 1154 and there are no further records of a castle at Downton.

GREAT BEDWYN CASTLE

Great Bedwyn was once a place of importance, with 28 burgesses in 1086 and a fine Norman church. The only mention of a castle is by Leland, c1540, who speaks of its ruins. Possibly he was referring to the Iron Age fort 1.2km to the north at Chisbury.

GREAT SOMERFORD CASTLE   ST 964832

The motte on the south bank of the Avon, SW of the church, may have been one of the castles built by Robert of Gloucester in 1144 to encircle Malmesbury. Excavations revealed a wall with a doorway and two round-headed windows, suggesting that Robert buried the original Norman parish church in his motte.

HORNINGSHAM CASTLE   ST 264513

NE of Woodhouse Farm, 1km WNW of Horningsham is a hilltop enclosure with traces of walls, including what looks like the base of a round tower or dovecote.

Ludgershall Castle

LEWISHAM CASTLE   SU 244739

High up on Aldbourne Chase, 2km SW of Aldbourne village, is a modest oval ringwork 40m in diameter with a ditch surviving on the west side. It may mark the site of a former hunting lodge.

LUDGERSHALL CASTLE   SU 264513   F

Edward, Sheriff of Wiltshire, probably had a house here at the time of Domesday Book (1086). By 1138, when Ludgershall was held by John the Marshall for the Empress Matilda, a ringwork had been added to what is thought to have been an Iron Age fort. Matilda fled to the castle after her attack on Winchester was repulsed by a relieving force sent by King Stephen but soon moved on to the stronger castle at Devizes. John had a long-standing feud with Patrick, grandson of Sheriff Edward, although he later married Patrick's sister, after which Patrick supported Matilda and was created Earl of Salisbury by her. By 1175 the castle was in royal hands, possibly because William Marshall had supported the rebellion of 1173-4, and it was visited by Henry II that year. The castle was given by Richard I to his brother Prince John but confiscated after John's rebellion in 1194. During his reign from 1199 John was a frequent visitor to hunt in the adjacent park. Small sums were frequently spent on maintenance, a chaplain is mentioned in 1202-3, and a new kitchen was ordered to be built in 1205. Nearly £38 was spent on repairs to the tower in 1211-12.

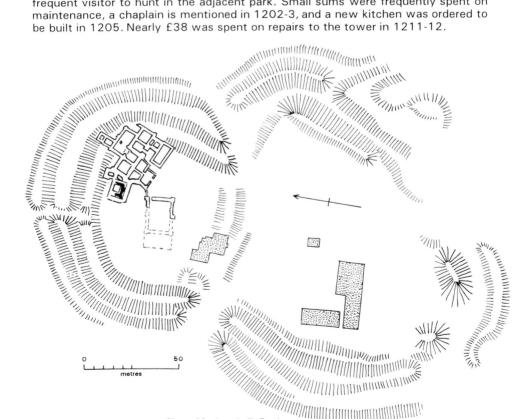

Plan of Ludgershall Castle

The castles of Ludgershall and Marlborough were held by William Marshall the younger from 1217 until returned to royal hands in 1222, when Henry III ordered new stables for both castles. In 1225 the gatehouse at Ludgershall was rebuilt. A new hall was erected in 1234 and the king's chamber was whitewashed, painted with lines and wainscotted, whilst stained glass depicting the Crucifixion with figures of St Mary and St John was inserted in the window at the head of the king's bed. The whitewashing of the chapels of St Leonard and St Catherine is also mentioned. A third chapel, of St Nicholas, is mentioned in 1241 when it was ordered to be re-roofed and whitewashed, whilst the queen's chamber was to be wainscotted and a porch was to be erected in front of the king's chamber. A new hall was ordered in 1244 and a gallery in front of the queen's chamber. A porch in front of the hall doorway was added in 1248, and a new kitchen in 1250, when the outer wall was rebuilt, whilst in 1251 a series of apartments were built for the use of Prince Edward, and frequent repairs to buildings are recorded throughout the 1260s.

William de Berkeley raided the estate during the conflicts of 1264 and there is a record of either Ludgershall or Marlborough (or both), having been strengthened with outworks (described as "bastions"), although excavations have shown that there was no curtain wall at Ludgershall and by this period it was purely a hunting lodge, no more defensible than the palace at Clarendon. The outer rampart was heightened, but probably more for viewing the gardens and estate rather than for defence. Henry's queen Eleanor held the castle in dower until her death in 1291, and it was often later held by queen consorts. A new chamber and chapel were built in 1285. In the 1340s £244 was spent on repairs to the gatehouse, the bridge in front of it, re-roofing the hall and the keep and building a new chapel and chamber. The castle was repaired by Henry IV's widow Joan of Navarre in 1422. The castle was later held by the Earl of Richmond and was then granted by Edward IV to his brother George, Duke of Clarence. When John Leland visited it c1540 the castle was said to be "cleane downe" although he noted the king's "pratie lodge" beside the ruins. The keepership had become hereditary in the Brydges family, later Dukes of Chandos.

The original egg-shaped enclosure 100m by 120m was defended by a double line of banks and ditches, except perhaps towards the village on the SE, which seems to have had its own enclosing ditch. Added to it was the northern enclosure about 80m in diameter also with a double line of ramparts and ditches although the inner rampart was later removed. On the north side a tower about 9m square still partly stands in a very defaced state to a height of 11m. It was probably built by King John to contain his private chambers over a lofty basement, and stands on a wider foundation thought to represent an earlier attempt to build a larger rectangular keep. The upper rooms were reached by a spiral stair in the NE corner and had fireplaces in the SW corner, which was strengthened by a round buttress. These upper rooms had latrines in a projection at the NW corner and had windows, probably of two lights, facing east and south. To the east of the tower are foundations of a contemporary private hall. It was remodelled and in the 14th century rooms were added on either side.

The main hall built by Henry III in the 1240s on the site of an older hall of c1200 lay further south in the middle of the ringwork. It was contained in a block about 20m long by 14m wide externally with buttresses clasping the corners and in the middle of the sides. Less than half of it has been revealed by excavation. Originally roofed with shingles, it was re-roofed with slates about a hundred years later. The hall was a very fine apartment divided by an arcade into east and west parts and having very lofty windows each of two lights with a transom and a quatrefoil in the head like the restored examples at Winchester. A gallery led from the NE corner to the more private lodgings. Service buildings lay to the east. The gatehouse mentioned in Henry III's accounts lay on the south side of the ringwork and was almost square in plan.

Ludgershall Castle

MALMESBURY CASTLE ST 934873

The town is almost surrounded by a loop of the River Avon and a tributary stream. The abbey lies in the unenclosed gap. Within the precincts lay a castle built in the 1130s by Roger, Bishop of Salisbury. It was captured in 1139 by King Stephen but then soon fell to a surprise attack by the Flemish freebooter Robert Fitz Hubert, although Stephen soon retook it again. The 30m diameter ringwork with a ditch on the south side on Cam Hill 1.4km SSE of the town (beside a footpath at ST 941858) is one of three siegeworks erected by Robert of Gloucester in 1144 to isolate Stephen's garrison. Matilda's son Henry captured the castle in 1153, aided by treachery within. In 1215 King John handed over the site to the abbot with permission to demolish the fortifications.

The motte at Marlborough

MARLBOROUGH CASTLE   SU 184687

This royal castle probably existed by 1070, when William I had Aethelric, Bishop of Selsey, confined at Marlborough and it certainly must have existed in 1110, when Henry I held his Easter court here. The castle was captured in 1138 by John the Marshall in support of the Empress Matilda, and strengthened. King Stephen was besieging the castle in 1139 when news reached him of his adversary the Empress Matilda having landed in England. Stephen's son Eustace attempted to capture the castle in 1149. Henry II confiscated the castle from John the Marshall and in 1158 made Alan de Neville its custodian. Rebuilding, probably in stone, was in progress during the late 1170s. On his marriage with Isobel of Gloucester in 1189 Prince John was given Marlborough and Ludgershall by his brother Richard I. Hubert Walter, Archbishop of Canterbury captured the castle at Marlborough from the rebellious Prince John in 1193. As king, John was a frequent visitor and had a new kitchen built in 1205 amidst other ongoing maintenance, Hugh de Neville being the keeper at this time. The castle was captured by the barons at the end of John's reign but in 1217 was recaptured by William Marshall for the young Henry III.

Henry III spent about £2000 on work at Marlborough castle. In 1224 a new tower of two storeys was built being the king's "leaded chamber". It was probably this tower which soon became cracked due to faulty foundations and required rebuilding in 1241-2, whilst the kitchen provided in 1250 may have been located in this tower. The 1220s also saw work on a new stable block, repairs to the hall and the provision of a brattice behind the queen's bedchamber, whilst a new chancel was added to the chapel of St Nicholas in 1229-30. A new chamber for the queen and a penthouse along the west side of the hall were ordered in 1244, a barbican was added to the gateway and a west tower to the chapel of St Nicholas in 1250, and in 1256 there were repairs to the curtain wall which had fallen in three places. The knights' chamber which cost £10 to erect in 1270 was probably timber framed. The castle was handed over to one of Simon de Montfort's supporters after the battle of Lewes but was recovered by its former castellan, Roger de Clifford, supported by a number of his fellow marcher lords.

The castle was later held in dower by various queen consorts and was a favoured residence of Henry III's widow Eleanor. The castle was occupied by the Despensers in 1321 but his opponents plundered the place in June and in September he was obliged to surrender it, although when executed in 1326 he was in possession. After a visit by Edward III and Queen Philippa in 1358 the castle decayed and in 1391 a commission decided that the apartments would need a complete rebuilding, which was never executed. Leland in 1541 found the castle a ruin. The Seymour family obtained the site and in 1620 Sir Francis Seymour erected a new house which was visited by Charles II in 1663, although nothing remains of it. Another new house was erected between 1699 and 1723 by the 6th Duke of Somerset. After the 7th Duke died in 1750 the house became an inn, but since 1843 it has been part of a college.

Rubble footings of the NW part of a shell wall with pilaster buttresses around a court 28m in diameter have been found on the summit of the 16m high motte which may have been raised over a barrow. The great tower mentioned in 1210-11 and completed c1238-50 seems to have been a circular keep within this shell wall, which is itself mentioned in 1194. The summit is now dished, thus hiding a water tank in the middle. The college buildings occupy the bailey, a platform 100m by 70m lying to the south which had moats fed by the River Kennet, which winds around the site to the south. The nature of this potentially water-logged site explains the need for good foundations. Traces of the bailey curtain have been found on the east side but nothing of the bailey defences is currently visible.

The site of Mere Castle

MEMBURY CASTLE   SU 305745

This is a very feeble rectangular enclosure 70m by 50 with a ditch along the north side. Excavations c1941 found the base of a possible 12th century tower keep underlying a 13th century house with a chapel. There is also evidence of a round tower, although this feature may have been a dovecote.

MERE CASTLE   ST 809325   F

Strongly sited on the east end of Long Hill, high above the village, was a castle which Henry III licensed his brother Richard, Earl of Cornwall to fortify in 1258. It had been abandoned by 1398. The castle had a rectangular court about 25m wide and 80m long with circular towers at the corners and in the middle of each long side.

NORWOOD CASTLE   ST 984945

By Dean Farm NW of Oaksey is an oval bailey 45m by 35m with the SW section of its ditch still wet. A small and low motte lies to the SE. South of Oaksey church are traces of the moat of a house of the Dukes of Lancaster which was ruinous by 1670.

The keep remains at Old Sarum

The palace at Old Sarum

OLD SARUM CASTLE   SU 138327   E

William I had a huge ringwork built in the centre of the oval Iron Age hillfort. There is a mention of the king's chamber in the castle as early as 1070 when he paid off his invasion army at this central point. In 1075 the bishop of Sherborne transferred to Old Sarum, although a new cathedral there was only begun after the king;s nephew Osmund became bishop in 1078. The new cathedral was consecrated in 1092 and a tower keep was added to the ringwork soon after Henry I's accession in 1100. Under the new bishop, Roger, elected in 1102, but not consecrated until 1107, the east end of the cathedral was extended and two new palaces erected, one each for the bishop and king. The castle was also given a stone gatehouse. Roger was later given possession of the castle but he fell out with King Stephen, who in 1139 confiscated all his castles. Stephen ordered the castle and part of the cathedral buildings to be destroyed by the sheriff of Wiltshire in 1153 but this does not seem to have been carried out before the king's death in 1154. The next bishop, Jocelyn de Bohun added towers to the cathedral west front and a south porch, whilst Henry II had the castle provided with a stone curtain wall. A wing was added in 1181-2 on the south side of the keep to house the royal treasury, but Henry II generally preferred to stay at his palace at Clarendon 5km to the SE which had a park attached to it.

By the end of the 12th century the clergy and castle garrison were at loggerheads. The clergy complained of a lack of space for expansion and a lack of water on their part of the hilltop. A plan to build a new cathedral and town on the level ground to the south was approved by Richard I in 1194 but it was not until an incident in 1217 when the clergy found themselves locked out by a garrison claiming to fear a foreign attack that the move went ahead. Bishop Richard Poore founded a new cathedral in 1220 which was mostly completed over the next thirty years, although nearly a century passed before completion of the spire. In 1226 the tombs of bishops Osmund, Roger and Jocelyn were transferred to the new cathedral and the old building was abandoned. Henry III took over the old bishop's palace, which was demolished for its materials in 1236. The old town was also gradually abandoned, and was deserted by 1540, although it continued to provide a member of parliament until 1832. The castle remained in use as the seat of the sheriff of Wiltshire. It was refortified during the war of the 1260s but soon decayed subsequently. In 1336 a group of prisoners managed to break out of it. The prison remained in use until Henry VI granted the castle to Sir John Stourton in 1447. Henry VIII allowed the groom of his chamber, Thomas Crompton, to remove materials from the castle in 1514 and that ended its useful life. Old Sarum became a national monument as early as 1892.

The east range of the palace at Old Sarum

The earthworks of Old Sarum are particularly impressive with ramparts of both the inner and outer lines of defence rising 16m or more above their ditches. Beyond the outer ditch is a counterscarp bank. The outer enclosure is 400m long by 340m wide and contains the foundations of the old cathedral in its NW quadrant. The cloister was rather unusually located in the angle between the north transept and the choir. The bishop's palace was set around a court between it and the outer wall, for the whole hilltop was stone-walled by the late 12th century, except perhaps the NE quadrant left incomplete probably as a result of Bishop Roger's fall from power and death in 1139. One small fragment of the wall stands beyond the cathedral site. There were gates to west and east, the latter being the most important.

The castle bailey measures about 90m across and is enclosed by the lower part of a late 12th century curtain wall up to 3m thick. Around the southern part pilaster buttresses occur on the outer face every 10m or so. On the east side is a gatehouse about 12m square but with the walls extending further east beyond the outer arch, where there is a drawbar slot. A high turret adjoined the gatehouse SW corner. The passage is flanked by guard chambers in the wall-thickness. Originally these were vaulted over. The well near the palace has never been cleared to its anticipated full depth of about 60m. A second well lies further south.

The early 12th century palace lies on the north side of the bailey. It contained four ranges around a courtyard at an upper level. The west range contained the main hall and the north range the great chamber or more private hall. The private apartments in the east and south ranges had latrines in a turret on the east side. Service rooms, including a kitchen lay in a lower storey on these two sides only, and a tower projected north from the NE corner onto the rampart. The chapel of St Nicholas formed the SE corner of the apartments, and there was a more public second chapel below it. This chapel, of St Margaret, had a vaulted ceiling. Perched on the rampart NW of the palace is are slight remains of the contemporary Herlewin's Tower.

The palace was entered through a forebuilding at the SW corner. The keep on the
west side of the bailey was reached from there by some steps further west, up into
a vestibule over a postern gateway passage closed by two doors with drawbars. The
keep measured about 17.5m square over walls up to 3m thick above a battered
plinth. The walls were originally faced with green sandstone blocks but most of these
were later removed for use elsewhere. The keep had a crosswall dividing each storey
and contained a hall and chamber side by side over dark basements above an earth
infill of the base of the tower. Latrines were provided on the south side and there was
probably a chapel over the entrance vestibule, an arrangement found in many other
keeps. A treasury 6m square was later added at the east end of the south wall. Only
footings remain of a bakehouse built by Henry III south of the main gateway and even
less of the new hall SE of the keep which he had rebuilt in 1247.

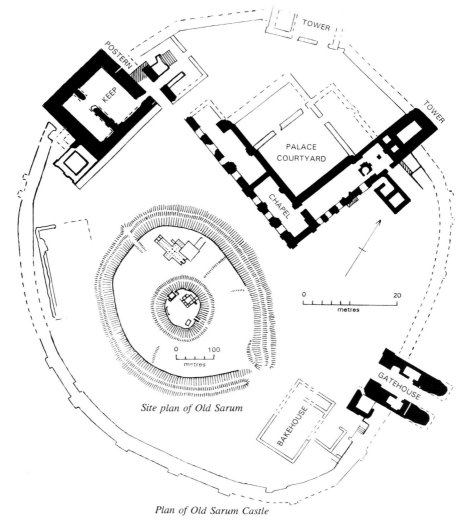

Site plan of Old Sarum

Plan of Old Sarum Castle

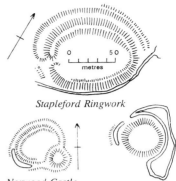

Stapleford Ringwork

Silbury Hill

Norwood Castle

Sherrington Motte

SHERRINGTON MOTTE   ST 960393

On the south bank of the River Wylye, west of the church, is a 6m high mound with a summit 28m across. Except on the west it is surrounded by a wet moat up to 15m wide. Traces of a bailey ditch 8m wide have been found 110m to the NW. The castle is thought to have been built by Osbern Fitz Giffard in the late 11th century.

SILBURY HILL   SU 100685   F

This huge prehistoric mound commanding a Roman road has slight evidence on the summit that it was fortified, even if only briefly, some time during the 11th or 12th century. Excavations in 1968 found an early 11th century coin and evidence of a rampart with a vertical timber revetment.

STAPLEFORD CASTLE   SU 068378

An oval ringwork 90m by 60m beside the River Till has a rampart and ditch around its northern perimeter. This part faces a rectangular enclosure 220m by 150m with a rampart and ditch but of little defensive strength. A fishpond lies on its SE side. Within the ringwork are signs of possible foundations of walls.

STOURTON CASTLE   ST 769319

At the end of a wooded ridge beside the boundary with Somerset is a motte with a summit 30m across on which are footings of a small tower keep. Beyond a rock-cut ditch on the west a bailey platform 30m wide extends 60m and has a ditch along its west and north sides. An outer enclosure lies to the north. There is a possibility that there was a later medieval fortified house closer to Stourton village, which was itself superseded by the Hoares' 18th century mansion of Stourhead.

TROWBRIDGE CASTLE   ST 855580

Amongst the centre of the town east of the River Biss is the site of a strong and important castle which is first mentioned in 1139 when it was held by Humphrey de Bohun and withstood an attack by King Stephen. In the 13th century the castle was refortified in stone with seven towers. Although repaired in 1375, it was probably little used during the 14th and 15th centuries, being described in 1468 as derelict. The inner bailey measured about 80m by 60m and had a motte, perhaps added later, in the NW corner. A much larger outer ward lay to the north.

WARDOUR CASTLE   ST 938263   E

In 1393 Richard II granted a licence to John, 5th Lord Lovel for the crenellation of his house at Wardour. John, 7th Lord Lovel, was a Lancastrian and consequently lost part of his estates, including Wardour, on the accession of Edward IV in 1461. The castle was briefly held by Lord Audley and then the Earl of Kent and then was held by Edward IV's brother George, Duke of Clarence until his execution and attainder in 1478. It passed to Thomas Butler, Earl of Ormond, who leased it to Lord Cheyne and then in 1499 sold it to Robert, Lord Willoughby de Broke, a kinsman of Lord Cheyne. Some time after the death of his son the succession was disputed and the castle eventually passed to the Grevilles, who sold it to Sir Thomas Arundell. After his conviction for felony in 1552 the estate was sold to William Herbert, Earl of Pembroke, although the castle was still occupied by tenants. In 1570 Sir Matthew Arundell, son of Sir Thomas, repurchased the castle and in 1578 began to remodel it as his own residence. His son Thomas was made a Count of the Holy Roman Empire for his services at the siege of Gran in Hungary and in 1605 James I made him Baron Arundell of Wardour.

In 1643 a Royalist garrison of twenty five men plus a few female servants held the castle against a 1300 strong Parliamentarian force led by Sir Edward Hungerford and Colonel William Strode. After a few days the castle was damaged by mining and the defenders forced to surrender. The castle was plundered, its furniture carried off, the pictures burnt, and the 3km length of piping which brought water to the site was cut up and sold. Henry, 3rd Baron Arundell, who had recently succeeded when his father Thomas died of wounds, brought up a Royalist force against the castle but was unable to take it. However a Royalist siege was maintained against the place from December through to March 1644, when Edmund Ludlow and his garrison of seventy-five men surrendered. The main gate was blocked during the siege and the castle badly damaged by mining and cannonfire. Two of the angle turrets fell, together with part of the roof. In 1652 the 3rd baron forfeited his property but it was purchased by a friend and then recovered at the Restoration. The family still own the castle, although since 1936 the ruin has been in state guardianship (now English Heritage).

Wardour Castle

Wardour Castle

The courtyard of Wardour Castle

The castle at Wardour takes a very unusual form. The main apartments are contained within a hexagonal structure 31 m in diameter overall with outer walls 1.8m thick. The rooms are grouped around a central court 12m across in the centre of which is a well. Some 50m away from this central structure was a thin outer wall, mostly rebuilt in the 16th century, which enclosed a bailey containing outbuildings. Vaulted rooms remain on the south side, and the pavilion on the SW, dating from the landscaping of the grounds in the 18th century, may stand on the site of an outer gatehouse. The bailey was commanded by higher ground to the NE, where the grotto now lies, and it does not appear that any attempt was made to defend this enclosure during the Civil War sieges. An underground passage linked the east side of the main building with the outer wall, allowing escape in case of attack. The NE side of the main castle projects out, since it is wider and has towers at either end. The lofty main hall is located here and it reached by a flight of steps from the inner court, through a fine doorway of the 1570s with Tuscan columns and lion masks in the spandrels. The hall has fine two light windows with transoms high up in the outer wall, a 16th century fireplace on the other side, and a mural room on each side. These contained machinery for winding portcullises, for the main entrance passage, originally fan vaulted, lies below the hall, with store-rooms on either side and a small porter's lodge on the north. The outer arch of the entrance was remodelled in the 1570s when this side was refaced, and there are niches on either side, behind which are blocked medieval loops. The outer portcullis was then done away with, but in the 1640s a makeshift portcullis was installed by cutting into the entablature and columns of the new doorway. The south end of the hall was screened off as a service passage (over which a gallery was later provided) and has access to two service room in the southern tower, plus a stair leading both up and down. One of the service rooms has a hatch and doorway through to the kitchen extending up through two storeys within the SE range. The hall intrudes into the north tower and beyond there is only a narrow space, thought to have once been a chapel.

The north range contained the lord's hall over a fine vaulted room. Here probably was the extremely expensive black marble fireplace overmantel destroyed by the Parliamentary troops. The other three ranges of the castle have lost most of their outer walls. They provided extensive private lodgings on four levels, since the presence of latrines shows that even the lowest rooms were for living or sleeping in. There were many lodgings formed of pairs of rooms comprising a living room and a bedroom provided with a latrine. An inventory of 1605 mentions 35 rooms within the castle. The inner walls of the south and SW ranges were mostly rebuilt in the 1570s. Many new windows were inserted in the outer walls at that time, most of them of three lights. At the summit of the building was a boldly moulded cornice, above which rose turrets over the stairs in the corners of the towers flanking the entrance, and hexagonal turret on the other four corners, although only one of these now survives. An 18th century drawing suggests that the main parapet was plain and only the turret parapets were embattled.

WEST DEAN CASTLE   SU 256275

In woodland east of the church are traces of an enclosure about 60m across once enclosed by a ditch up to 12m wide. The rampart was probably flattened to form the bowling green recorded here in the 19th century. Outworks may have extended out around the church itself.

WILTON CASTLE

SU 100310

King Stephen in 1143 converted a nunnery situated west of the site of Wilton House into a castle.

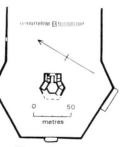

Wardour: site plan

Doorway at Wardour Castle

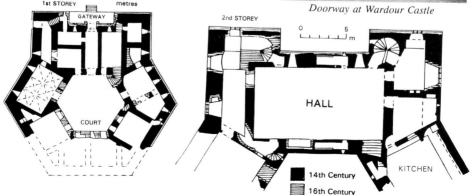

Plans of Wardour Castle

A GLOSSARY OF TERMS

ASHLAR - Masonry of blocks with even faces and square edges. BAILEY - defensible court enclosed by a wall or a palisade and ditch. BARBICAN - Defensible court, passage or porch in front of an entrance. BASTION - A projection in front of (but not rising above) the outer wall of a fortress. BLOCKHOUSE - A very small fort. BUTTERY - A room where drink was stored. CAPONIER - Covered passage in a moat to provide flanking fire or access to outworks. CASEMATE - Vault under a rampart to accommodate guns or personnel. CORBEL - A projecting bracket to support other stonework or a timber beam. CURTAIN WALL - A high enclosing wall around a bailey. FOREBUILDING - A fortified porch containing the entrance to a keep and sometimes also the stairs leading up to it. A chapel was often provided above. HERRINGBONE MASONRY - Stones laid diagonally in zig-zag courses. JAMB - A side of a doorway, window or other opening. KEEP - A citadel or ultimate strongpoint. The term is not medieval and such towers were then called donjons from which word is derived the word dungeon, meaning a strongroom or prison. LIGHT - A compartment of a window LOOP - A small opening to admit light or air or for the discharge of missiles. MACHICOLATION - A slot for dropping or firing missiles at assailants. MOAT - A defensive ditch, water filled or dry. MOTTE - a steep sided flat-topped mound, partly or wholly man-made. MULLION - A vertical member dividing the lights of a window. PARAPET - A wall for protection at any sudden drop. PILASTER BUTTRESS - A shallow buttress like a rectangular attached column PLINTH - The projecting base of a wall. PORTCULLIS - A wooden gate (sometimes sheathed in iron) made to rise an fall in vertical grooves, being hoisted up by means of a windlass. POSTERN - A back entrance or lesser gateway. RINGWORK - An embanked enclosure of more modest size than a bailey, generally of greater width but less elevated than a motte summit. SHELL KEEP - A small stone-walled court built upon a motte or ringwork. SOLAR - A private living room for the lord and his family. STRONGHOUSE - A mansion not fully equipped for a sustained defence against a proper siege but difficult for malefactors to break into or burn down because of its solid walls and moat. WARD - A stone walled defensive enclosure.

PUBLIC ACCESS TO THE SITES

E Buildings in the care of English Heritage. Fee payable at some sites.
F Ruins or earthworks to which there is free access at any time.
O Buildings opened to the public by private owners, local councils, trusts, etc.
V Buildings closely visible from public roads, paths, churchyards & open spaces.

FURTHER READING

Norman Castles in Britain, Derek Renn, 1968
Castellarium Anglicanum, D. Cathcart King, 1983
A History of the King's Works, several vols, 1963-70
The Victoria Counties of Dorset, Hampshire, Somerset, Wiltshire (several vols each)
Royal Commission on Historical Monuments Inventories for Dorset (several volumes)
Buildings of England series: volumes for Dorset, Hampshire, Somerset, Wiltshire.
Pamphlet guides or monographs are available for Basing, Bishop's Waltham, Calshot, Carisbrooke, Christchurch, Corfe, Dunster, Farleigh Hungerford, Hurst, Ludgershall, Nunney, Old Sarum, Porchester, Portland, Sherborne, Southampton, Southsea, Taunton, Titchfield, Wells Palace, Wardour, Winchester, Wolvesey, and Yarmouth
See also articles in the Archaeological Journal, Chateau-Gaillard, Country Life, Fortress, Medieval Archaeology, and the annual transactions of the various county archaeological societies and field clubs.